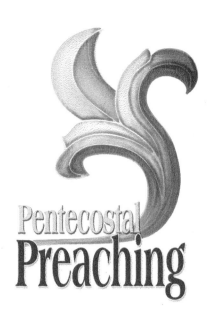

Pentecostal
Preaching

D1523297

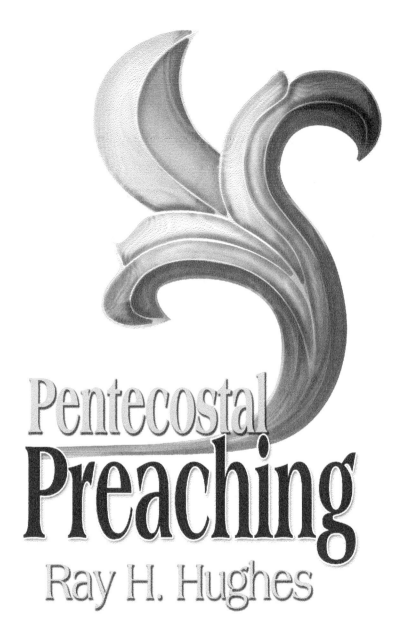

Pentecostal Preaching

Ray H. Hughes

Pathway

P R E S S

Scripture quotations are from the King James Version
of the Bible.

Book Editor: Wanda Griffith
Editorial Assistant: Elise Young
Inside Layout: Mark Shuler

Library of Congress Catalog Card Number: 2004109275
ISBN: 0-87148-085-9

Revised 2004

Pathway Press
Cleveland, Tennessee

Introduction

Ray H. Hughes' book, *Pentecostal Preaching*, comes at an opportune moment. The worldwide Pentecostal, or charismatic, revival shows signs of continued growth. It is becoming more obviously the cutting edge of that greater movement often referred to as *Evangelicalism*, and Pentecostals are impacting social and church institutions with an influence undreamed of even a decade ago.

The many books presently being published on the subject, not to mention magazine articles and editorials, clearly indicate unabated interest and enthusiasm for understanding Pentecostals and for grappling with what makes them so vital a force in today's world.

Dr. Hughes offers no new explanation of this phenomenon—as with others, he attributes the miracle of the revival entirely to the work of God's Holy Spirit in human lives—but he does approach the subject from a somewhat different perspective. From notes, sermon outlines, and personal experiences accumulated over a period of more than 60 years, he bares his heart and shares his thoughts in a manner that will be interesting to those who agree and even to those who disagree with his primary thesis.

Seldom has an author seemed more ideally tailored for his subject. Ray H. Hughes was born March 7, 1924, the son of a pioneer Pentecostal preacher. He accepted Jesus Christ as personal Savior when he was only 9 years old. With his ministry now in its 64th year, he has effectively served his church as evangelist, pastor, state overseer, and general executive official. He distinguished himself as a youth leader when he served as general youth and Christian education director of the Church of God; as an educator when he served as president of Lee College; and as a denominational leader by having been twice elected general overseer of the Church of God.

Ray H. Hughes' prowess as a Pentecostal preacher has been recognized for years, both within and without his own denomination, and he has served as special speaker in many interdenominational gatherings, including four Pentecostal World Conferences.

Those who know him best, especially those who have followed his ministry closely, feel he stands forth most clearly as an evangelist. He has always been, and he yet remains, a man whose heart burns with an unusual burden for the lost. In moments of reflection, he admits that God called him to be an evangelist; and, without doubt, evangelism has characterized every facet of his ministry for four decades.

Thus it seems that in terms of background experience, in terms of personal success when it comes to preaching, and in terms of having heart and feeling for what can be accomplished through preaching, he is ideally suited to speak on this subject. While there have been many voices raised in praise or in defense of the Pentecostal experience, there has been little written or said about Pentecostal preaching itself.

The reader will notice at once that Dr. Hughes has a clear definition of what Pentecostal preaching is. His is a concept that encourages the minister to study and to become the best instrument possible, while at the same time allowing for the free flow of God's Spirit both in the speaker's life and in every pulpit performance. At the same time, his is a concept that is anchored firmly in God's Word and allows no place for frivolity or for those excesses sometimes laid to the charge of Pentecostals.

In this book you will find no simple answers and no one-sentence explanations. You will find no trite efforts to show one how to become a successful Pentecostal preacher. Ray Hughes' respect for all those complex elements that merge to make preaching effective is too great for that. What you will find is a second-generation Pentecostal's effort to balance and to counterbalance those many factors that have been part of his ministry for years; an effort that at times may be both cutting and thrilling; and an effort that always rings with conviction and a sense of mission.

You may find some surprises in this book. You will surely complete it with a better understanding of what it means to accept the call of God and to step forth as a gospel preacher in the spirit and power of Pentecost.

While you may not agree with everything Ray H. Hughes says in terms of Pentecostal preaching, you will not deny the attractiveness of his concepts and you may well rejoice that he believes and writes convincingly of the possibility of such preaching in today's world.

And . . . such preaching being possible . . . you may feel strangely inclined to see what God can and will do in your own life.

Hoyt E. Stone

Table of Contents

1

The Power in Pentecostal Preaching

Introduction

Few people deny there is power in preaching. Men of the pulpit have wielded an awesome power and influence over our world for centuries. The pulpit has shaped and reshaped social, political, economic and educational values. Preachers have made their local pulpits famous. They have often moved from behind their pulpits into the activities of a broader public arena.

Some men are by nature endowed with human talent which allows them to speak effectively, to organize well, to lead others, and to succeed in the business world. The popularity and the success of such men need not always be attributable to the intrinsic power of preaching. By the same token, some of these men make poor impressions in public life, they may live out their days without popularity or fanfare. But it need not be concluded that the intrinsic power of preaching is missing from every such man's pulpit.

One must not confuse earthly power, human power, and the power of speech and persuasion with the real power of preaching, although these traits may on occasion go hand in hand.

There is basic, intrinsic, divine power in preaching itself. This power is of supernatural origin. It is present with or without the human factor, with or without popularity, with or without fancy trimmings, with or without public acceptance or acclaim.

The real power of preaching does not reside in men, nor does it redound to human praise. This is not to say that human talent is of no value in the life of a minister. This is not to imply that training, education, or any number of obvious individual characteristics will not contribute to the overall success of what the Church is attempting to do; it simply notes that aside from the human element, away from the training and the education, in spite of the strength or the weakness of the instrument, real preaching retains a power of its own.

Three elements combine to produce the power of preaching: the Word, the Holy Spirit and interaction between pulpit and pew.

The Word of God

The foundational power of preaching resides in the Word itself. This power is inherent in the Word. It is a power no human effort can remove and no demonic influence can defeat. Power resides in the Word.

God's Word is the product of the Holy Spirit. Prophets of old spoke and wrote as they were moved upon by the Holy Spirit. Historically, the New Testament church began when Christ gave Himself on Calvary, purchasing the church with His blood. In this same historical sense, God's Word existed before the church.

The Word was given to the church as a guide for its
operation, as a message for its members, as a standard
for its doctrines, and as a medium for its experience.

The church is not the lord of the Scripture, because
the church did not make the Scripture. "What? came
the word of God out from you? or came it unto you
only?" (1 Corinthians 14:36). The church was shaped
by the Word and can only exist and maintain its vitality as it abides in, and operates according to, the commandments and the doctrines of the Word.

Jesus Christ placed the Word in its proper perspective in His life and ministry. He was prolific in the use
of scriptures in His teaching and preaching. He
expounded the Scriptures relative to things concern-
ing Himself (Luke 24:27). He called upon His hearers
to "search the scriptures" (John 5:39). He spoke "as
one having authority" (Matthew 7:28). He used the
Scriptures to substantiate this authority, for the "scripture cannot be broken" (John 10:35). The Word is eternal; it will never pass away (Matthew 24:35). This is
why Jesus repeatedly said, "It is written." Jesus knew
the power of the Word and that the devil could not
stand against it.

Nothing can be plainer or more startling than the
appeal which Jesus Christ made to Scripture as the
ultimate authority on every question. Although He is
the fulfillment of Scripture, He recognized the Holy
Spirit as the real and responsible Author.

A look into the Book of Acts readily reveals the centrality of the Word in the New Testament church. The
Word was fully preached.

> Then they that gladly received his *word* were bap-
> tized (2:41).

Howbeit many of them which heard the *word* believed (4:4).

And now, Lord, behold their threatenings: and grant unto thy servants, that with all boldness they may speak thy *word* (v. 29).

We will give ourselves continually to prayer, and to the ministry of the *word* (6:4).

And the *word* of God increased; and the number of the disciples multiplied in Jerusalem greatly; and a great company of the priests were obedient to the faith (v. 7).

Therefore they that were scattered abroad went every where preaching the *word* (8:4). Now when the apostles which were at Jerusalem heard that Samaria had received the *word* of God, they sent unto them Peter and John (v. 14).

While Peter yet spake these words, the Holy Ghost fell on all them which heard the *word* (10:44).

But the *word* of God grew and multiplied (12:24).

And the *word* of the Lord was published throughout all the region (13:49).

Paul also and Barnabas continued in Antioch, teaching and preaching the *word* of the Lord, with many others also (15:35).

And he continued there a year and six months, teaching the *word* of God among them (18:11).

So mightily grew the *word* of God and prevailed (19:20).

> And now, brethren, I commend you to God, and
> to the *word* of his grace, which is able to build
> you up, and to give you an inheritance among
> all them which are sanctified (20:32).

This quick overview of the Book of Acts points out that the early church was Christ-centered, Spirit-dominated and Word-based. All the members were continually spreading the Word of God, honoring the Word, and explaining the Word. The Word of God constituted the message and became the authority for all claims of the church. The Word of God was the source of all preaching. It was the standard for all doctrine. And it was the medium of all experience. So must it be today if men of the pulpit will have power in their preaching.

In a very definite sense, the preacher today is a trustee of the Word. "But as we were allowed of God to be put in trust with the gospel, even so we speak; not as pleasing men, but God, which trieth our hearts" (1 Thessalonians 2:4). In order to preach the Word, of course, the man of God must be acquainted with it. He must meditate upon the Word. He must assimilate the Word into every part of his life.

In writing to young Timothy, Paul said,

> Till I come, give attendance to reading, to exhor-
> tation, to doctrine. Neglect not the gift that is in
> thee, which was given thee by prophecy, with the
> laying on of the hands of the presbytery. Meditate
> upon these things; give thyself wholly to them;
> that thy profiting may appear to all (1 Timothy
> 4:13-15).

The preacher in today's world must have the same attitude Job had: "I have esteemed the words of his mouth more than my necessary food" (Job 23:12).

David hid the Word in his heart (Psalm 119:11). Jeremiah was told that the Word of the Lord would be like fire in his mouth (Jeremiah 5:14).

Too often it seems that ministers today reverse the apostolic approach and give themselves to tables rather than to the Word. Because they deal in small and frivolous matters, we have famine in the land, not a famine of food but, as Amos said, a famine of the Word (Amos 8:11). Men deal with abstracts. They propound their own philosophies. They deal with human speculations, rather than with great and noble truths of the Bible.

When men root their preaching in the soil of the Bible and eat often from the fruit of its bounty, there is an inexhaustible supply of truth at their disposal. In the Word, the preacher finds thoughts that breathe and words that burn. Give a Bible to a man who knows its content and who understands basic methods of study, and he will never be wanting for a sermon.

Charles Spurgeon, who wrote prolifically and who preached many sermons, once said, "There are hundreds of texts in the Bible which remain like virgin summits whereon the foot of a preacher has never stood. After 35 years I find the quarry of Holy Scripture inexhaustible. I seem hardly to have begun to labor in it."

If the preacher will stay with the Scriptures, he will avoid the error of pulpit trifling. Men go astray and the pulpit is rife with heresy because preachers do not search the Scriptures. Jesus said to the Sadducees, "Ye do err, not knowing the scriptures, nor the power of God'" (Matthew 22:29). Paul wrote, "For whatsoever things were written aforetime were written for our learning, that we through patience and comfort of the scriptures might have hope" (Romans 15:4).

The minister who would preach and who would have power in his preaching must know beyond the shadow of a doubt that the Bible is the Word of God. When we say that the Bible is the Word of God, we mean that it is inspired of God. It is God-breathed. "All scripture is given by inspiration of God, and is profitable for doctrine, for reproof, for correction, for instruction in righteousness: That the man of God may be perfect, thoroughly furnished unto all good works" (2 Timothy 3:16, 17).

The term interpreted here as "inspiration" denotes a forcible respiration, a strong, conscious inbreathing; it is God speaking through men. The Bible is the Word of God just as much as if God spoke every single word of it with His own lips, (2 Peter 1:21).

The Bible is not founded on argument. It is not justified by logic, though its logic is obvious. The Bible is a series of messages by witnesses, those who spoke with the authority of the Holy Spirit. When men look to the Bible as the Word of God, they marvel at its unity. The Bible contains one system of doctrine from cover to cover. Always its doctrine is consistent. Such unity is impossible if one views the Bible as a human book. The Bible was written by 36 to 40 authors, their compositions spread over a period of 1,500 years. These writers came from all classes of society, yet the Word blends into a unity.

As it stands today, the Bible is a miracle. This can be explained only by the fact that there was one Author behind the human authors, one Spirit inspiring many writers. When the Word of God again increases in our pulpits, the number of disciples will multiply. Great companies of men and women will turn to the faith and many people will be added unto the church.

The apostle Paul, that wise master-builder, admonished the young pastor of Ephesus to "preach the word" (2 Timothy 4:2). Paul knew the Word was quick and powerful, alive and energizing. He understood the Word would not return void but would accomplish what God pleased and that it would prosper in the things whereunto God sent it. Paul knew the Word would turn men from darkness to light, from the power of Satan unto God. He knew it was the revelation he had received from God and that it was more necessary than food for his mouth. Paul had come to trust the power of the Scriptures as he reasoned daily in the synagogues.

The ministry and the laity of this day need to stay in the Word. When this is done, the church will reap not the fruit of human labors, but the fruit of what the Word can produce.

The power of God's Word transcends the centuries. In it are ideals for this generation and this age. When the faithful old book lies folded in golden silence on the pulpits of the world; when the earth has turned white-hot and then cooled to a cinder; the Word shall yet stand. When time shall be no more and when all men stand before their Maker, the book shall be opened and men shall be judged by the Word. Men ought to preach the Word.

The real power of preaching—the inherent, foundational power of preaching—rests forever in the Word.

The Holy Spirit

Just as the Word is the foundational power of preaching, so the Holy Spirit is the operational power of preaching.

No matter how many gifts are manifest in a minister's life, the major element which attests that he is truly called is the power and anointing of God upon his preaching. The anointing adds a forcefulness to his message which ordinary speech, however eloquent, would never carry. Paul expressed it in these words:

> For our gospel came not unto you in word only, but also in power, and in the Holy Ghost, and in much assurance; as ye know what manner of men we were among you for your sake (1 Thessalonians 1:5)

> For the preaching of the cross is to them that perish foolishness; but unto us which are saved it is the power of God (1 Corinthians 1:18)

> For I determined not to know any thing among you, save Jesus Christ, and him crucified. And I was with you in weakness, and in fear, and in much trembling. And my speech and my preaching was not with enticing words of man's wisdom, but in demonstration of the Spirit and of power (2:2-4).

> For the kingdom of God is not in word, but in power (4:20)

Here, the most gifted of the apostles clearly recognized that his preaching success lay not in his intellectual prowess, nor in his innate persuasive ability, but in the power of the Holy Ghost to convince men and to awaken them to regeneration. The commission of Paul was to "turn them from darkness to light, and from the power of Satan unto God" (Acts 26:18). Paul knew this could never be accomplished in his own strength. It had to come through the power of the Holy Ghost. It is the Holy Spirit which makes alive. The Holy Spirit is as indispensable to preaching success as water, air, and food are to the human body. Without the Holy Spirit, the minister's office is mere name and his position powerless. If he does not possess the Spirit Jesus promised, he cannot perform the commission Jesus gave.

Jesus made it clear in His references to the Holy Spirit that the Spirit's word would be multifaceted. The names applied to the Spirit further emphasize the many areas in which, and through which, the Holy Spirit works: He is Comforter, Guide, Leader, Baptizer, and the Spirit of truth. He is the Source of power and the One who will bring all things to our remembrance.

Unfortunately, some ministers equate the anointing with loudness, demonstration, or certain pulpit mannerisms. Others think of the Spirit's work only in terms of pulpit performance. They act as if, when it comes to study and preparation, the Holy Spirit takes a leave of absence; or as if He somehow shuns the study room or the prayer closet.

Preaching begins with study and preparation. There, too, we have God's Holy Spirit to assist and to guide. Paul classified ministers as workmen (2 Timothy 2:15). Solomon noted that "much study is a weariness of the flesh" (Ecclesiastes 12:12). It has been said that man has approximately nine billion brain cells, but that the average man puts only from seven to nine million of them to work. It would seem there is a lot of lost motion going on in some of our minds. Ministers need to study and to prepare themselves for the preaching of God's Word. Adam Clarke said, "Study yourself to death and then pray yourself alive."

It seems obvious that a preacher must first prepare himself before he prepares his sermon. This comes through prayer and communion with almighty God, through reading the Word, through assimilating its truths, through meditating upon its promises. Preaching is not just a performance; it is the aggregate of a lifetime. It is the outflowing of a man's soul that follows his personal infilling. It is Jesus Christ revealed through the human instrument.

The Word of God is the preacher's manual. "Study the Bible in the mornings," Theodore Cuyler said, "and study doorplates in the afternoons." Paul said to Timothy, "Give attendance to reading, to exhortation, to doctrine" (1 Timothy 4:13). Some ministers simply lack the personal discipline required for study. They wonder why their preaching lacks power, but they will not saturate themselves in the Word.

This brings us rather naturally to the old excuse that studying bores, that it lacks the excitement of street work or personal confrontations. Yes, study may at times be difficult; but if one brings God's Holy Spirit as partner into his study, things liven up and one finds himself on a mental and spiritual adventure comparable to none other. In those hours when the minister is alone with the Scriptures, he needs the enlightening power of the Holy Spirit. Knowing the author always make a book more interesting and understandable. The Holy Spirit is the Author of the Word.

Why is it that sometimes we read a passage of Scripture and see nothing? Again, we read the same verses and the words seem to jump off the page. The Spirit makes the difference. When a man retires to his study and opens the precious Bible, before he reads a passage or makes a note, he should put his soul and heart in tune. With the Holy Spirit. The Spirit brings light and understanding.

It is the Spirit, as well, who helps men to rightly divide the Word of God. Without the Spirit, without being in touch with the Author of the Word, men tend to read their own private thoughts into the Word. Men find in Scripture a justification for pet ideas or projects. Thus, they become guilty of prostituting the pulpit and handling the Word deceitfully. "For we are not as many, which corrupt the word of God: but as of sincerity, but as of God, in the sight of God speak we in Christ" (2 Corinthians 2:17).

Unless one can rightly divide the Word, he does not truly understand the Word. It is here where men very much need the Holy Spirit, for He is the Spirit of wisdom and the Spirit of understanding.

Preachers need the wisdom of the Spirit to know how to choose the appropriate portion of Scripture in the first place. While some men stoop to mere "text hunting," or pick up a catchy phrase from just any place, the man who preaches with power is one who seeks the Spirit's wisdom first in the choosing of the passage and then in the proper interpretation and application of that text to his listeners. No man is worthy of the name *preacher* who does not select his themes under the guidance of the Holy Spirit. It is here where many sincere preachers struggle most—knowing what to preach and when. If God has ordered a message and one applies it to himself, then that message is bound to be effective. Any other route veers from the New Testament pattern, a practice which eventually leads to lifelessness and failure.

Beautiful are those moments when the man of God steps from the pulpit and is met by a man or woman who says with tears, "You'll never know how much those words meant to me. That sermon was for me. God spoke through you to my heart."

Just as God inspired Peter in the choice of his text from Joel, so God can and will lead preachers today in choosing and preparing in the moment of decision. The Holy Spirit is omniscient. He knows all things at all times. In one's study on Monday, or any other day of the week, it is the Holy Spirit who knows precisely who will be in the congregation next Sunday morning. When the Spirit directs, the message will be sharp and powerful.

Although the Spirit illumines and warms the heart in the study and in the prayer closet, it is in the actual delivery of the sermon that the Spirit's work is most obvious. It has been aptly said, "The anointing makes the difference."

What is the anointing of the Holy Spirit? It is something we speak of quite glibly, but it may be, at the same time, something which some misunderstand. Some people confuse human expressions or mannerisms of the anointed with the anointing. For example, the anointed preacher may speak rapidly and in a loud, excited voice; but loudness and excitement are not in themselves the anointing of God's Spirit.

There is a difference between inspiration and the anointing of the Holy Spirit. Men sometimes feel inspiration. Artists are inspired to paint, writers to write, and politicians to wax warm on their favorite themes. It is altogether likely that some men preach—and preach quite well, in human terms—solely from human inspiration. But inspiration is not necessarily the anointing of the Holy Spirit.

The Holy Spirit also can inspire. Even though the opposite is not always true, the anointed preacher will most assuredly be an inspired preacher. Most of us have our favorite types of speakers, as did New Testament believers (see 1 Corinthians 1). We enjoy listening to some preachers more than to others. Some men are more logical, some more easily understood, some more pleasing in terms of voice or style; but we ought not confuse human attributes or talents with the anointing of God's Spirit. Many popular speakers are loud and boisterous. God may choose as well to anoint men who are of a quieter disposition.

There is, and there always will remain, something mysterious and miraculous about preaching. In the pulpit, under the anointing of God's Spirit, men often speak and act beyond themselves. There are times when a word of knowledge, a word of wisdom, or a revelation comes to the preacher right out of heaven.

Men who preach under the anointing of God's Spirit understand the importance of research and study. They know the value of preparation in terms of the heart and the head. They know even more certainly that it will take the Holy Spirit to make their words live. It is the Spirit that burns in the soul and which so often, and many times unexpectedly, turns a sermon's minor point into the primary thrust of the message.

During times of exceptional anointing, new sermons are born. What was meant to be only one point is enlarged upon by the Spirit, and thus later becomes a sermon in itself or even a series of sermons. This is why a man should not be bound to an outline or manuscript. During the anointing, God often opens up a fresh avenue of thought; and, if one is bound to his notes, he will not experience the thrill, adventure and joy of discovering new territory for preaching. He will never ascend those lofty heights of spiritual revelation known to the man who preaches with openness to the Holy Spirit. This type of preaching requires total dependence upon the Spirit. While it is more rewarding, it is also humbling. One is ever-conscious of the fact that God is in control.

This viewpoint of preaching does not question the propriety of using an outline, or even a manuscript. The Spirit of God can and should rest upon a preacher when he prepares the outline and manuscript. The point emphasized is that place must be given in every sermon for prophetic unction of the Holy Spirit. The preacher should always go into the pulpit with David's words ringing in his ear, "I shall be anointed with fresh oil" (Psalm 92:10). When preachers literally get caught away and enraptured in the power of the Holy Spirit, Jesus is magnified and glorified. The human instrument is reduced and the Christ of glory is exalted. That is preaching as God intended, the power of the gospel cutting like a two-edged sword.

My grandfather was a blacksmith, so I spent some time in blacksmith shops during my childhood years. I noticed that the blacksmith can do virtually no work without fire. Until the iron is hot, the blacksmith's hammering and beating does little more than produce a few sparks. With the fire, however, the hardest steel becomes pliable in the blacksmith's hands.

Preaching is similar. It takes fire to bend, to mold and to reshape people. It takes fire to make human instruments pliable. Otherwise, the preacher wastes his energy and gets only sparks for his trouble.

Joseph Parker was once asked if he ever preached an old sermon. "No," he replied with a smile, "but I've never hesitated to repeat a new one."

Alexander Maclaren said he could never preach an old sermon as such; he had to give it hot.

Others have spoken on this same subject. Ian Macpherson noted, "A slack bow speeds no arrow. An unstrung violin yields no music. And the minister who merely stands up in cold blood to read his discourse rarely reaches the heart." Spurgeon said, "We ought to be driven forth With abhorrence from the society of men for daring to speak in the name of the Lord if the Spirit of God rests not upon us."

Guy Duffield put it this way, "I believe there is a way in which we can preach the Word of God so that, when folk may have forgotten what we said, they will not forget what God has said; and the Spirit of God will again quicken that Word, and anoint that promise and instruction to their hearts whenever the tests or the trials come."

Duffield goes on to say that the Holy Spirit anoints a man to preach in a distinct, twofold way: "One, the Spirit makes truth which has been studied to pulsate with new life; two, the Holy Spirit helps a man to preach better than he knows."

James Forbes Jr. said: "More is happening when you stand to do your thing than meets the eye. Are you prepared to swing with it and to expect it and to be open to it? If not, then again you cut off at least two thirds of what the Lord is able to do when the Word is proclaimed in faith."

So it is with some men when they go into the pulpit. Their study becomes a chain of bondage. They are enslaved to the outline, or to some preconceived notion as to where they are going, and they find it difficult to flow with the Spirit. God forbid! It is the Holy Spirit, Author of the Word, who transforms the thoughts and words of a man into sharp arrows of salvation.

The Pulpit and the Pew

Preaching must center in the Word. Preaching must be anointed of the Holy Spirit. But preaching also must be conscious of the connection between pulpit and pew.

"It is at his peril that the preacher loses touch with his hearers," Ian MacPherson wrote, "For they have it in their power either to make or to mar his message."

Speaking along this same line, John Watson is even more explicit. "A supercilious or frigid people," he said, "can chill the most firey soul, while a hundred warmhearted folk make a plain man eloquent."

Since it is understood that the minister stands between man and God, at least in the communicator sense, then it becomes every preacher's responsibility to stay in touch with both. The man of God cannot become so cloistered, so withdrawn, so enraptured of heavenly things that he loses touch with where people live and hurt. God's man cannot spend so much time in the marketplace of life that he fails to cultivate the spiritual contact that makes him burn with holy zeal. He must strive to become a blend of the two extremes.

MacPherson advises the preacher to "observe carefully alike the performance of the preacher and the response of the congregation notice how the one evokes the other; and draw deductions there from which will stand you in good stead in days to come." His is an interesting observation. Most of us accept easily that the preacher evokes response from the congregation, for such is a primary objective of preaching; but in what way does the congregation play upon the preacher?

Have you ever wondered why a minister preached so much better during camp meeting or at some mass rally than to a small gathering? Or maybe you have noticed the opposite. Some men speak better, more lucidly, before a small crowd than before a large one. Truth is, the congregation does affect the preacher.

Two observations seem important at this point.

First, some men are by talent, by training or by nature more comfortable with smaller crowds. They speak and they approach their ministering with an intimacy that goes best in such a setting. Enlarge the crowd and their rate of efficiency drops. These men are often very successful and in no wise should their calling be disparaged.

Second, just as a minister can know personal inspiration which has no direct link to the Holy Spirit, so can a minister draw human inspiration from an audience, which may or may not have anything to do with divine order. Crowds cheer on their favorite athletes. Similarly, some men play to the grandstand while preaching. They tickle ears. They major in catch-phrases. They appeal to prejudice and the carnal passions of their listeners.

A man's preaching cannot be judged solely on the basis of crowd enthusiasm, or in terms of how well people like him. There is, however, New Testament example and clear reason for believing that preaching should be done with a proper blending of these elements. On the Day of Pentecost, Peter stood up with

the 11 disciples and ministered to the astonished congregation. It should be observed that when Peter
stood up to preach, the Eleven stood with him. At this
first Pentecostal church service, the whole church par-
ticipated in the sermon. In true Pentecostal preaching,
the congregation and the minister act together. The
minister preaches, but the congregation responds and
supports the message.

Simon Peter spoke as one having authority and
conviction. The message was simple but effective. It
complemented the testimony of the believers and
resulted in an overwhelming response by the unbelievers. Pentecostal preachers preach for a response;
and, as a part of worship, Pentecostal people respond.
Perhaps for this reason many Pentecostal sermons
conclude with the congregation around the altar seeking God. Such preaching points men to God; and, in
response to the Word, men seek God's face.

One should be careful, though, to resist the ever-
present temptation to respond negatively when a congregation is less than enthusiastic. The Word of God is
sharp. It cuts. People do not shout and rejoice when
they are undergoing spiritual surgery. One must
always be conscious of the men and women to whom
he speaks, but one is not to predetermine what their
response ought to be. A passage of Scripture which
makes one man rejoice, may at the same time force
another to his knees. The Holy Spirit that anoints one
to speak is the same Holy Spirit that applies the Word
to the hearts and lives of listeners. Preachers must
submit to His will. God's man must permit the Spirit
to work unhindered and must not retaliate or become
resentful because the congregation does not respond
as he thought they would.

A lot of the pastoral brutality—the harsh ministerial attitudes displayed in some pulpits today—come about because the preacher has not been in touch with the Lord. He has not had his heart broken and his soul overwhelmed with compassion before attempting to speak for God. Some men are indignant rather than inspired, when they preach. Some speak out of prejudice rather than from spiritual conviction. Such preaching is unworthy of the name. It is the mark of a hireling. "For the pastors are become brutish, and have not sought the Lord: therefore they shall not prosper, and all their flocks shall be scattered" (Jeremiah 10:21).

Summary

God's man is to preach the Word. He is to preach under the anointing of the Holy Spirit. He is to preach with the needs and the lives of his listeners always in mind.

As James Forbes has said: "When we go into the pulpit, let us expect that, when preaching is done, the same kinds of things that happened in the New Testament days will happen for us. Have we ever been interrupted in our sermons like Peter was at Cornelius' house? If we are not sometimes interrupted in our saying it by the Lord's doing it, then we need to look at our preaching again."

The intrinsic power of preaching stems from the Word. The activating power of preaching is God's Holy Spirit. How these two factors blend to produce the transforming power of a Pentecostal sermon is determined by the spiritual connection, the unity of purpose between pulpit and pew.

2

The Place of Pentecostal Preaching

Introduction

Preaching is the primary responsibility of every minister. Paul felt the urgency of preaching so strongly that everything else in the ministry was secondary. Paul wrote, "Christ sent me not to baptize, but to preach the gospel" (1 Corinthians 1:17). Because it is the saving medium, the preeminent work in Paul's life was to preach the gospel, "For though ye have ten thousand instructors in Christ, yet have ye not many fathers: for in Christ Jesus I have begotten you through the gospel" (4:15).

Many people do not comprehend what is involved in preaching the gospel. The dictionary definition of preaching places it on a level with other forms of public speaking. *Preaching* is defined as another form of propaganda. Ours is such a day of mass production and mass communication that there is even danger of preachers themselves treating the subject lightly.

Many responsibilities crowd in on today's preacher, tending to obscure the main burden of his call; but, whatever a minister's special gift, his first obligation is to proclaim the gospel. The apostle, prophet, evangelist and pastor are all called to preach. Preaching is not just an adjunct to the saving activity of God: it is the heart of this activity. Paul set forth its significance when he said, "It pleased God by the foolishness of preaching to save them that believe" (1 Corinthians 1:21). Preaching is the God-chosen medium of man's salvation.

Throughout the New Testament are a number of words which indicate phases of the ministry of preaching. The two most prominent words are *euaggelizo* and *kerusso*. It is from *euaggelizo* that we derive the words *evangel* and *evangelist*. The word means "to announce good news, to declare, or to bring glad tidings." Jesus used this term in the opening declaration of His ministry: "The Spirit of the Lord is upon me, because he hath anointed me to preach the gospel" (Luke 4:18).

The word *kerusso* means "a proclamation from a throne," giving it the connotation of a message being delivered on behalf of a sovereign. Paul used this word when he wrote, "I keep under my body, and bring it into subjection: lest that by any means, when I have preached to others, I myself should be a castaway" (1 Corinthians 9:27). *Kerusso* connotes a message of authority, implying that the one delivering it has been delegated the responsibility by someone else. The preacher's message is not his own but the message of the King.

Some sermons serve primarily to teach the saints; some elaborate on a social issue; and some expound the historical lessons of the New Testament. These may be good and needed, but every minister should know and remind himself that the gospel of Christ, which is "the power of God unto salvation" (Romans 1:16), refers to Christology, to the doctrine of Christ as Savior of the world; and the minister should examine himself periodically to make sure that he builds his sermons around this basic framework.

In his book *Pentecostal Preaching*, Guy P. Duffield Jr. observes: "Preachers should make sure they deliver a message rather than that they merely preach a sermon. There is a world of difference. A message should be a sermon, but not every sermon is a message." Later, when we discuss the role of the Holy Spirit in preaching, we will comment further on this subject.

Preaching has always been placed center stage in the life and history of the church. We now propose to examine that place within the context of four points:

- Preaching in the life of Jesus
- Preaching in the New Testament church
- Preaching throughout the history of the church
- Preaching in today's world

Preaching in the Life of Jesus

The public ministry of Jesus spanned approximately three years. The nature of His ministry was threefold: (1) preaching and teaching; (2) exorcism (the casting out of devils) and healing; (3) the training of disciples.

Paul described the ministry of Christ in capsule: "And without controversy great is the mystery of godliness: God was manifest in the flesh, justified in the Spirit, seen of angels, preached unto the Gentiles, believed on in the world, received up into glory" (1 Timothy 3:16).

While it would not be correct to limit our concept of ministry to preaching alone, it is nevertheless true that preaching played a prominent role in the life of Christ. Jesus explicitly stated that He came to preach (Mark 1:38, 39). Jesus preached His first sermon in His hometown, at the synagogue, and on the Sabbath. He used Isaiah's Messianic prophecy as His text:

> The Spirit of the Lord God is upon me; because the Lord hath anointed me to preach good tidings unto the meek; he hath sent me to bind up the brokenhearted, to proclaim liberty to the captives, and the opening of the prison to them that are bound; To proclaim the acceptable year of the Lord (Isaiah 61:1, 2).

Matthew tells us, "Jesus went about all Galilee, teaching in their synagogues, and preaching the gospel" (4:23).

Mark says He was preaching and casting out devils (1:39).

Luke simply writes, "He preached in the synagogues of Galilee" (4:44).

While Jesus said He came to preach, He was also recognized as a master teacher. In the life of Christ especially, I believe there was a degree of overlapping between preaching and teaching. Through teaching, Jesus expounded in detail that which He came to proclaim. Within the Gospels, there does not always seem to be a sharp distinction between preaching and teaching. Preaching can be called the foundation and teaching the superstructure. Every building must have both.

One does find, however, some noteworthy and distinguishing qualities in the preaching of Jesus.

Jesus spoke with authority. The scribes were as dry as dust. They dealt with trivia, tradition, ceremony and legalism. They spent their time with minutiae. They quibbled about nonessentials and majored in minors. Jesus spoke with such authority that men were astonished and amazed at His doctrine. Jesus did not speak as a mere commentator, parroting or echoing the message of men long dead; nor did He feed His listeners on skeletal sermons of the past. He spoke spiritual realities, divine truths, as the voice of God to the people.

All classes of people came to hear Christ preach. His fame spread abroad. Pharisees, doctors of the Law, publicans, sinners, common people—all heard Him and concluded, "Never man spake like this man" (John 7:46).

Luke wrote, "The people pressed upon Him to hear the word of God" (5:1). Mark recorded, "Many were gathered together, insomuch that there was no room to receive them, no, not so much as about the door: and he preached the word unto them" (2:2).

Jesus spoke as a prophet. Those who came to hear Him recognized in Jesus Christ the great order of the prophets. They said He spoke as one of the prophets. His words were so forceful some believed Him to be one of the old prophets raised from the dead. Later, others speculated that He was John the Baptist raised up.

The message Jesus preached was straightforward and uncompromising. He joined issue with the world, the flesh and the devil. He never hesitated to speak against corruption and hypocrisy, whether among religious leaders or politically powerful families. The "lily of the valley" was also the "lion of the tribe of Judah." The Lamb who was meek and gentle could also be provoked to wrath.

Jesus preached under the anointing of the Holy Spirit.
The Holy Spirit came upon Jesus at the beginning of
His ministry, following His baptism in the Jordan
River. It was evident that He went forth in the power
of the Spirit to preach. John declared, "For he whom
God hath sent speaketh the words of God: for God
giveth not the Spirit by measure unto him" (John 3:34).
Jesus had the Spirit without measure, the full anointing, and the enduement of power from on high. He so
testified when He said, "The Spirit of the Lord is upon
me" (Luke 4:18).

The apostle Peter recognized that Jesus ministered
through the power of the Holy Spirit: "God anointed
Jesus of Nazareth with the Holy Ghost and with
power: who went about doing good, and healing all
that were oppressed of the devil; for God was with
him" (Acts 10:38).

Along with these three distinguishing qualities in the
preaching of Jesus—His speaking with authority, His
speaking as a prophet, and His anointing with the Holy
Spirit—note the form and the style of His preaching.
Surely some of the attractiveness of Christ's preaching
can be attributed to His style. Most of our Lord's statements were pithy, pointed, crystalline words. What He
said was simple easily understood and easily remembered. Paul spoke later of the simplicity that was in
Christ. What Jesus said was at the same time profound
and thought-provoking. His words evidenced that He
loved people and had a desire to communicate.

Jesus used many illustrations. Jesus compared truth
with the common objects of the countryside, with the
skills of farming, thus relating to the people of that

setting. He preached where people lived. Jesus took listeners from known objects to new realities. He was descriptive in His presentation and this left His congregation in awe. Jesus depicted scenes from the surrounding landscape. He related to the housewife by talking of cups and platters, lamps and candlesticks. He related to working people by speaking of mills and millstones. In terms of everyday life, He mentioned a mother sewing a piece of new cloth onto an old garment, and a father straining wine into skin bottles.

Jesus was a man of the street, of the countryside, of the marketplace. Because He filled His sermons with such language, He won the hearts of the people.

Jesus was adept in the use of parables. Toward the latter days of His life, parables became so much a part of the Lord's preaching and teaching that they have become inextricably linked with His ministry in the minds of most people today. Although many people think parables originated with Jesus, they were also used in the Old Testament. The rabbis of Jesus' day also spoke in parables. Jesus used parables to simplify spiritual truths for believers. On other occasions, He spoke to conceal the truth from unbelievers. Unquestionably, Jesus refined the art of using such stories, and we could profit from His example today.

Jesus had content in His sermons. While the form of one's preaching is important, it is substance, or content, that is supreme. When Jesus came into the life of Israel, preaching was at a low ebb. The preaching of Jewish religious leaders was given to such things as the proper breadth of the phylacteries, the proper length of fasts, the articles on which one should tithe, the things by which one could be ceremonially unclean, and a thousand other tiresome details. When men's hearts grow cold and lukewarm, they always move away from the centrality of the gospel, drifting to the peripheral things and matters of little consequence.

Jesus dealt with relevant subjects. His sermons had content. We could never name all His subjects here, but a quick listing would include the following: the New Birth, the Water of life, the Resurrection and the Life, the Bread of life, the Light of the world, the door of the sheepfold, the promise of the Holy Spirit, the Vine and the branches and the last days.

As an example, let us look briefly at the Lord's Sermon on the Mount, one that has served as basis for thousands of discourses since.

The sermon opens poetically with what we call the Beatitudes, or the Psalm of Jesus. These ninefold beatitudes have no equal in all recorded literature. In them, Christ expressed His religious ideals. The great moral values set forth in the Beatitudes have been adaptable to every era of human history. In this sermon of 111 concise verses, Jesus dealt with the light of the world, the salt of the earth, evil desire, divorce, retaliation, hatred, ostentatious praying, improper giving, fasting for praise, anxiety, wealth and uprightness of character. The Sermon on the Mount is a little gospel all by itself, a superb example of how Jesus preached.

Today any man who would enter the Christian ministry, or any who would attempt to preach the gospel, should first acquaint himself with the preaching of Jesus Christ. Here is the perfect example. Recognize the principles involved. Keep the message relevant and the language simple.

Preaching in the New Testament Church

The New Testament church came into existence in the wake of two momentous events—the Resurrection and Pentecost. Just as the resurrection of Jesus Christ—a confirmed, proven, undeniable fact—provided the early disciples with unquenchable motivation for living, so Pentecost empowered them with holy boldness and zeal for taking the gospel to all men. The outpouring of the Holy Spirit was accompanied by a number of miraculous signs and wonders. "A sound from heaven as of a rushing mighty wind . . . cloven tongues like as of fire," men and women speaking "with other tongues as the Spirit gave them utterance," (see Acts 2), a multitude of people astounded because they heard simple Galileans speaking in their native tongues—these were the most notable events of the Day of Pentecost, phenomena of which we often speak and preach.

There was another miracle, the preaching of Simon Peter. Although we know he was commissioned and sent forth of the Lord, along with the other disciples, we have no record that Simon had preached before. It is likely Peter had done some teaching under the Lord's tutelage. Most certainly he had observed the Master's techniques and methods for communicating, with large crowds of people. At the same time, none would claim Peter was an experienced and eloquent public speaker.

Only a few weeks prior to this, Peter had cravenly denied even knowing Jesus of Nazareth. On the Day of Pentecost, Peter stood up, a stranger and a novice. The disciples who stood with him had no past example, no past performance on Peter's part, to make them feel comfortable with what he was about to say. Nevertheless, Peter preached: "Peter, standing up with the eleven, lifted up his voice, and said unto them, Ye men of Judaea, and all ye that dwell at Jerusalem, be this known unto you, and hearken to my words" (v. 14).

Peter's sermon was a masterpiece. It has been studied and copied and held forth as an example by all teachers since. Every preacher should acquaint himself with the fine points of Peter's sermon. For our purpose here, it is significant to note the church was launched through the preaching of a sermon.

The church continued to expand and to grow through preaching. In the third chapter of Acts, following the healing of the lame man at the Temple gate, a crowd gathered; it was here Peter preached his second sermon. Called before the Sanhedrin and questioned, Peter was so bold and outspoken that the learned men took notice he and John had been with Jesus. All true Pentecostal preaching exalts and honors Jesus Christ. In fact, Jesus is the main theme of Pentecost.

When threatened and placed in prison (5:18), the disciples continued to teach and to preach. When other matters called for attention, the disciples said: "It is not reason that we should leave the word of God, and serve tables. Wherefore, brethren, look ye out among you seven men of honest report, full of the Holy Ghost and wisdom, whom we may appoint over this business" (6:2, 3).

At least two of those first deacons soon left tables and launched their own preaching careers. Stephen preached and died with the message of Christ on his lips. Phillip preached in Samaria, then took good news to the Ethiopian eunuch. In the ninth chapter of Acts, Saul is filled with the Holy Ghost and anointed for ministry in Damascus. Paul stayed on for certain days with the disciples in Damascus, "and straight-way he preached Christ in the synagogues, that he is the Son of God" (9:20).

Peter preached to the Gentiles in the home of Cornelius (ch. 10). Paul and Barnabas were separated by the Holy Spirit, ordained by the church at Antioch through the laying on of hands, and sent forth to preach the Word of God (see 13:1-5).

While not all preaching recorded in the Book of Acts was done within a formal setting, not all sermons were delivered to large crowds, and not all sermons were tightly structured or fully recorded, preaching played a major and indisputable role in the growth and progress of Christianity. Those who went forth from Jerusalem and turned the world upside down were known first and foremost as preachers of the gospel.

Preaching Throughout the History of the Church

By the close of the Apostolic Era, approximately A.D. 100, Christianity had become established in a number of strong church centers throughout the Roman Empire. John the Revelator recognized some of the more prominent of these centers when he addressed letters to the "seven churches which are in Asia" (Revelation 1:4). It is from the next 100 years that some great names appear in church history: Clement of Rome; Barnabas, the fellow-missionary of Paul; Hermas; Ignatius, bishop of Antioch; Polycarp, bishop of Smyrna; and Papias, bishop of Hierapolis. These men were known for their preaching and their writings, as well as for their leadership.

In his *History of the Christian Church,* Qualben makes the following statement:

> Christianity spread with astonishing rapidity during the first three centuries. It spread to all parts of the Empire, even to regions beyond Roman territory. Christian missionaries found their way eastward to Mesopotamia, Persia, Media, Bactria, Parthia, India, and Armenia; southeast, to Arabia. it gained a firm foothold in Lower Egypt, especially in Alexandria; from there it spread to Middle and Upper Egypt; westward to the Roman provinces of North Africa. In Europe it spread to Gaul, up the Danube, and toward the Roman provinces in Germany. Tertullian (A.D. 160-220) holds that Christianity was brought to Britain toward the end of the second century.[1]

In seeking to explain why Christianity spread so rapidly, the same historian noted that these believers "were imbued with a strong conviction that Christianity was the only true and universal religion, the only means of salvation for mankind, and they preached accordingly."[2]

At the turn of the fourth century (A.D. 311 and 313), two imperial edicts granted religious freedom. Christianity did not become a state religion as such; but it received state sanction, persecution ceased, and many people began to endorse the Christian church without fully understanding or experiencing spiritual rebirth. As spiritual fervor declined, certain leaders advocated withdrawing from the masses, and monasticism came to the fore.

---

[1] *A History of the Christian Church,* Qualben, *80.*
[2] Qualben, *81.*

The church entered the Medieval Age. For the most part, church historians for this era concern themselves with the rise of the papacy, political conflicts within the church, and the setting forth of doctrines. Such tells us what the church was doing as an organization, it says little of what was taking place on local levels, among the common people. Let us remember, though, that this time period spanned many generations; and it is fair to assume that local preachers, teachers, evangelists and deacons continued to set forth the gospel story. Even secular historians point to the fact that it was the church during these dark years that preserved the educational system, which kept the light of knowledge burning, and which passed along the glorious message of Christ to parents and children alike.

Periodically, during this same period of time, itinerant preachers rose up, proclaiming the simple truths of Christ. Some of these men became quite popular; others were persecuted and rebuked by the ecclesiastical church. A number of prominent men preceded Martin Luther in condemning the papacy and in advocating a return to the simple gospel, but it was through Luther, Calvin and other reformers, that real revival came to the church.

Such men were known for their preaching. They spoke boldly, without fear, and with the anointing of the Holy Spirit, even though we have little historical evidence to document that they understood, as we do, the baptism of the Holy Spirit. We do know that they were preachers, that preaching was the instrument by which God's church came to revival and new life. Many of the sermons these great men preached are today a matter of record. Their sermons can be studied and read; and, within them, one finds the glorious gospel of Christ and His redemption.

Preaching in Today's World

It is not easy to evaluate the impact of preaching as one sees it in our world today. Book editors who solicit other materials often footnote their advertisements with the printed statement, "No sermons, please." Although the sermons of certain great men such as Spurgeon and T. Dewitt Talmage continue to be reprinted, it seems obvious that few men now command such attention. Even some of the mass-media evangelists, including the so-called electronic-church preachers, leave something to be desired. Many of these men give more attention to fund-raising and personal experiences than to the gospel of Christ. Others hype personal projects and business proposals which do not necessarily compliment the Christian ministry. Some have associated themselves with pet political aims and objectives.

Nevertheless, it is this author's opinion that this is, or should be, the golden age of preaching. Not only do opportunities abound, but the preacher of today has many methods and tools by which his sermons can be disseminated: radio, television, the printed page, cassette and compact disks recordings, to name a few. We also have videotape and closed-circuit television, and low-frequency stations, all opening more doors of opportunity for the preacher. God intends that His messengers make use of all possible means for spreading the gospel.

Ours is also a day of growing churches, of many public gatherings, of hospital and prison chapels, and so on, offering enterprising men opportunities to obey the Great Commission. One may come up with many excuses for not preaching in today's world, but lack of opportunity cannot be one of them.

Summary

Preaching ought not be judged altogether according to its popularity, its form or structure. Such judgments, normally made by men of this world, parallel all too closely the spirit of this age.

God does not so judge preaching. The New Testament gives many examples of preachers who were not popular, although one cannot conclude that popularity of itself is sinful. Phillip preached to great crowds in Samaria; he also expounded the Word to a lone man in the desert. Paul was persecuted and run out of many towns for his preaching. Early disciples were put in jail, some even sentenced to die.

In the final analysis, a man's preaching must be evaluated by something other than worldly acclaim.

Faithfulness to the Word, the centrality of Christ, the anointing of the Holy Spirit, the love and compassion with which the message is delivered, relevancy to the times and to the conditions of the listeners—these are some of the points from which evaluation can be made more accurately.

After all, it was Jesus himself who informed us that a soul is more valuable than all the treasures of this earth. God's men preach for heavenly gain. The gospel is good news to all men everywhere: it is life to those who hear, receive and believe. Today, as always, preaching plays a prominent role in the life of the church. It is at the heart and soul of God's plan for redeeming sinful men; and those who carry the message must never lose sight of the fact that preaching is a serious responsibility.

3

The Person and Pentecostal Preaching

Introduction

One needs but a cursory examination of the Bible to discover great variety in terms of the people God called into the ministry and in terms of the ministry God called them to perform. Jeremiah was a weeping prophet, Elijah a firebrand. Amos was a shepherd, Hosea a betrayed husband. Jonah was a reluctant preacher, Nehemiah an eager missionary. Where in all literature can you find two men more differently constituted than Peter the Rock and John the Beloved? Yet, both were called and loved of the Master. Both were men of rare and beautiful graces.

Although it is conceivable that God could have done otherwise—He could have sent angels with the message or He could have written it boldly in the clouds—God chose to use individuals, human instruments, in the preaching of the gospel. God chose to use men and women as they are in terms of personality, character and talent. God does not insist that ministers become robots, that they mimic some precise pattern, that they blindly mouth a prescribed sales pitch; but only that they give Him devotion and show a willingness to obey and follow the leading of His Spirit.

In the opening chapter, we noted that the power of preaching centers in the Word, made alive through the Holy Spirit and translated through the pulpit to the pew. Then we discussed the place of preaching in the divine scheme of things. It is now time to look at the preacher himself—the person, the instrument—through whom God chooses to work His will among men.

Indeed it is true that men contribute to the shape and success of their ministries. Men are not mere cogs in the wheel: they are vital factors in the formula. Without men the work suffers. Through dedicated men, miracles and unbelievable things happen.

The late J.F. Rowlands is a good example. Called into the ministry as a young man and especially burdened for the Indian people of South Africa, Rowlands spent 52 years in a ministry, which resulted in thousands of men and women coming to know Jesus Christ. At the same time, his ministry bore the imprint of Rowland's personality as surely as did his signature upon a check.

The apostle Paul talked in personal terms when he referred to his ministry. He spoke of "his" call and of "his" servanthood, personalizing it and admitting to the challenge and the responsibility. Paul referred to his converts as "my work in the Lord" (1 Corinthians 9:1) and "the seal of mine apostleship" (9:2). He called Titus "mine own son after the common faith" (Titus 1:4), and he called the gospel "my gospel" (Romans 2:16).

No man will be successful in the ministry unless he comes to this personal knowledge. The Word is eternal and dynamic. God's Holy Spirit is available and powerful. But God also needs a human vessel. At this point the person comes into the picture. "If a man therefore purge himself from these, he shall be a vessel unto honour, sanctified, and meet for the master's use, and prepared unto every good work. Flee also youthful lusts: but follow righteousness, faith, charity, peace, with them that call on the Lord out of a pure heart" (2 Timothy 2:21, 22).

Three areas of thought seem pertinent:

• The preacher and his call
• The preacher and his self-concept
• The preacher and his pitfalls

The Preacher and His Call

God calls men into the ministry. True, the call may come in various forms, under diverse circumstances, and at any time; but the successful preacher knows beyond a doubt that he is called of God. The method by which this conviction gets into a man's heart is relatively unimportant—some men have given glowing testimonies of visions and dreams and miraculous calls, and then turned aside into oblivion; others have taken up the Word quietly, with little fanfare, and have faithfully followed the Master—but it is important that the call burn white-hot and that the preacher can always turn to this truth for consolation and strength. People do not always please or praise. Circumstances do not always contribute to the minister's peace of mind. Desired evidences of success do not always accompany the preacher's labor. He must nevertheless hold a firm conviction of his calling or he is doomed.

The apostle Paul knew his ministry was a divine appointment. He was an apostle according to the will of God, by the effectual working of divine power. Paul did not choose to be a minister; he was chosen and given the privilege. Paul wrote to Timothy, "I thank Christ Jesus our Lord, who hath enabled me, for that he counted me faithful, putting me into the ministry" (1 Timothy 1:12).

Paul's perception of his call encompassed such phrases as "a steward of mysteries . . . a bond slave," "a servant of the people," and "an ambassador for Christ." More awesome yet, Paul confessed that a dispensation of grace had been committed unto him (see 1 Corinthians 9:17). His was a conviction dramatically expressed when he said, "Woe is unto me, if I preach not the gospel!" (v. 16).

Jesus preached, taught, performed miracles and went to the cross: but He also called men, sending forth the Twelve (see Mark 6:7-13) and the Seventy (see Luke 10:1-12), and centering His last words to the newly formed church in the Great Commission (see Matthew 28:18-20). Any man worthy of the ministry must first look into the face of Jesus and hear His straightforward, unequivocal command, "Take up . . . (your) cross daily, and follow me" (Luke 9:23). There are no substitutes for certainty of the call.

While one's initial calling may be rather subjective— who can argue with a man who has seen a vision, or dreamed a dream, or heard a voice from heaven? There are accompanying evidences of the call by which ministers are judged and evaluated. In so far as possible, church leaders are responsible for seeing that ministers give proof of their calling. Paul wrote to the young Timothy, "Be thou an example of the believers, in word, in conversation, in charity, in spirit, in faith, in purity" (1 Timothy 4:12).

Strength of character, honesty, purity, holiness—these are first and foremost evidences of the call of God. Whatever call a man may profess, if he has not been called to holy living, he certainly has not been called to the Christian ministry. A minister's chief necessity is holiness. Paul said to his fellow workers in the church at Corinth, "We . . . beseech you also that ye receive not the grace of God in vain . . . Giving no offence in any thing, that the ministry be not blamed" (2 Corinthians 6:1, 3).

Those whom God calls will be men who exercise wisdom and common sense in their relationships with other people. The New Testament church insisted even that deacons be men "honest . . . full of the Holy Ghost and wisdom" (Acts 6:3). James wrote, "If any of you lack wisdom, let him ask of God, that giveth to all men liberally" (1:5).

A calling to the ministry does not make one immune to errors in judgment, nor does it place one on some exalted plane wherein he no longer makes mistakes; but it should be substantiated by character.

When and if a man's life is marked by foolishness; when he constantly and continually sows confusion; when he leaves in his wake more hurt than healing; when he evidences none of the wisdom and the grace of Christ and of the early apostles of the church; then that man's calling should be questioned. The call of

God presupposes grace or moral qualification. It also implies a gift of ministry. If these are absent, then one's calling is in doubt.

Ministers live in a fishbowl; their every move observed and often commented upon. It is not unusual that the minister becomes an object of gossip. When called upon to make hard decisions, especially, or when led of God's Spirit to cut deeply into where people live, such gossip may be extremely painful. It is here that the minister must choose between the human inclination to track gossip down and root it out-in other words, to get even—or to console himself in the call of God, leaving the matter for eternity and the Judge of all things. Wisdom will decide.

There will be times when the man of God is very lonely, when he feels that no man cares. He may wrestle with anxiety or find himself in a state of serious depression. Such valleys hinder ministers and affect their performance in the pulpit, just as they hinder the spiritual journey of any other. But the inner conviction, the certain knowledge that God gives direction, God is the Employer, God is the Judge. In other words, "the call"—this is the beacon that steers God's man through the darkness and permits him to sing and smile when there seems no earthly reason for doing so.

The Preacher and His Self-Concept

To a great extent, the manner in which a preacher perceives himself will determine the joy and success in his ministry.

Some preachers think of themselves more highly than they ought. They condescend to preach. They preach down to people. They are egocentric. They emphasize "I." In doing so, they separate themselves from the flock they are called to shepherd and from the lost they are commissioned to save. Paul said, "For we preach not ourselves, but Christ Jesus the Lord; and ourselves your servants for Jesus' sake" (2 Corinthians 4:5). "Christ sent me . . . to preach the gospel: not with wisdom of words, lest the cross of Christ should be made of none effect" (1 Corinthians 1:17).

A minister must be willing to be made all things to all men that he might win some. When D.L. Moody was at the height of his success, it was said that "he acted as though he had never heard of himself." Preachers who are great really do not know it: they do not perceive themselves in that light at all.

At the same time, some men see themselves as inferior, second-rate, destined to failure. They never stand up, never launch out, never risk everything. The flesh profiteth nothing, it is futile, it cannot please God; but God has entrusted the gospel to men, allowing them to exercise certain talents according to His will.

Ministers must have enough confidence in Him to believe that He undergirds His called ones and qualifies them for the task. Call and qualification can never be looked upon as separable. While the call does imply a gift of ministry, the gift must be rekindled and cultivated. "Certain individuals have failed here by turning to empty argument" (1 Timothy 1:6, *Moffatt*).

The best view of a proper self-concept is found by looking at Bible examples. In the opening verses of the Philippian letter, Paul refers to himself as a servant. That certainly is an unauspicious title, not at all designed to commend him to men of this world. The word Paul uses is *doulos.* It means "a slave; one having no individual status but who is the property of his master." The minister must know he is not his own but that he is bought with a price. He is the workmanship of God, created in Christ Jesus.

Paul was a university graduate with first-rate theological training. He was a linguist who had been tutored by Gamaliel, a famous doctor of the law of Moses. Yet, throughout his ministry, Paul seldom mentioned such matters: he always referred to God's grace and to his personal confrontation with Jesus Christ on the road to Damascus.

Jesus was Master of all, but He perceived Himself as a servant (see Luke 22:27). John opened his record of the Revelation by acknowledging himself as God's servant. James, the Lord's own brother, began his epistle, I, "James, a servant of God and of the Lord Jesus Christ" (1:1). Jude began his epistle in a similar fashion (v. 1).

Nevertheless, these men were not timid or backward. They were not fearful or reluctant to step forth and speak. Paul set forth the proper attitude when he declared, "I can do all things through Christ which strengtheneth me" (Philippians 4:13).

God's man sees himself as a servant, but he is also an ambassador. He is charged with an assignment, and he must go forth in faith. Strangely enough, a man's attitude toward himself and his call will also color his attitude toward the circumstances of life. Since it is God who worketh in us, both to will and to do of His own good pleasure, then faith looks beyond the immediate circumstances and lays hold on the promises of God.

Many ministers today preach circumstances rather than God's message of faith and hope. They become embroiled with their people, thus allowing opposition to enter into the message rather than letting the message convert the opposition. Some seek to rebuke and to correct their people rather than permitting the Word to do its assigned task: "All scripture is given by inspiration of God, and is profitable for doctrine, for reproof, for correction, for instruction in righteousness" (2 Timothy 3:16).

How one perceives himself—whether the emphasis is centered in things heavenly or earthly; whether he considers himself God-called or just church-employed will help determine a man's success in the Christian ministry.

The Preacher and His Pitfalls

Some ministers do not make it. They turn out to be hirelings; they backslide; they bring shame to the church, to themselves and to all who vested them with confidence. There is little point in trying to explain why this happens or in arguing theologically whether or not the call was genuine in the first place: it is significant that this happens. Thus, it seems important that we discuss the pitfalls of the ministry.

We have made the point already that a man's life— how he lives and conducts himself; his honesty, purity and holiness—becomes the cutting edge of the preacher's influence. This may not always be immediately obvious, but it eventually shows up. While it has been said of a preacher that, "When in the pulpit he preached so well it seemed a shame he should leave; but, when out, he lived so bad it was a shame for him to go back," we can rest assured that such a paradox in real life brings only shame. God will judge. Jesus pronounced woe upon any who would offend one of His little ones: how much more terrible the retribution held in reserve for those who prostitute and make mockery of the gospel.

Of its very nature, a pitfall is something hidden and unseen. We may describe the elements involved in pitfalls, but we will not be able to remove them or to make those who read of them immune to those dangers inherent in the "wiles of the devil." One should not imply that the following list is in any way full and complete. Hopefully, it will warn, and provide food for thought.

1. *The minister must beware of vain glory.* Ministers play important roles in the lives of many people, and in the towns and communities where they serve. It is natural and understood that, by and large, ministers are held in high regard. In the 21st century, this may not be as true as it was for most of our nation's history. There is still, in some parts of our culture, a tendency to idolize ministers, to think of them too highly; but the minister ought not permit this to derail his own sense of devotion and commitment. Few things are more obnoxious, and at the same time more pitiful, than the sight of a man who encourages his followers in their carnal and worldly idolizing of himself. Some preachers do this. They are on an ego trip.

Paul wrote, "Let us not be desirous of vain glory, provoking one another, envying one another" (Galatians 5:26).

Joseph had the right attitude when he stood before Pharaoh, and was complimented and praised: "And Joseph answered Pharaoh, saying, It is not in me: God shall give Pharaoh an answer of peace" (Genesis 41:16).

The psalmist said, "Not unto us, O Lord, not unto us, but unto thy name give glory, for thy mercy, and for thy truth's sake" (Psalm 115:1).

Peter was confronted with this temptation at the height of success, just after the healing of the lame man; but he said, "Ye men of Israel, why marvel ye at this? or why look ye so earnestly on us, as though by our own power or holiness we had made this man to walk? The God of Abraham . . . hath glorified his Son" (Acts 3:12, 13).

A similar incident occurred when Peter arrived at the home of Cornelius: "And as Peter was coming in, Cornelius met him, and fell down at his feet, and worshiped him. But Peter took him up, saying, "Stand up; I myself also am a man" (10:25, 26).

When a man lame from birth was healed during the ministry of Paul and Barnabas at Lystra, the people rushed into the streets and proclaimed the two apostles Greek gods, Jupiter and Mercurius. They prepared to offer sacrifices in the street. Observing what was happening, Paul and Barnabas rent their clothes and ran into the crowd, shouting, "Sirs, why do ye these things? We also are men of like passions with you, and preach unto you that ye should turn from these vanities unto the living God, which made heaven, and earth, and the sea, and all things that are therein" (14:15).

Whatever the minister is, he is of God's divine grace and favor. He must never accept in any fashion the glory and praise which is due only to God.

2. The preacher must not secularize the ministry. For many years, polls indicated that ministers rated at the top of America's list of most respected professionals, putting them ahead of physicians and lawyers. This is no longer the case, due largely to the public moral failure of high-profile televangelists. This underlines the fact that ministry must never be thought of simply as a profession. It must not become a mere job, a perfunctory or ordinary task which a man can routinely perform. When such happens, the ministry is secularized, preachers lose their passion for souls, and the church exists as a social or civic institution rather than as the living body of Christ.

The minister always faces the temptation to stoop in this direction. Paul said to Timothy, "Neglect not the gift that is in thee, which was given thee by prophecy, with the laying on of the hands of the presbytery" (1 Timothy 4:14). First and foremost, the preacher must follow the example of the early apostles who said, "We will give ourselves continually to prayer, and to the ministry of the word" (Acts 6:4).

In his charge to the elders of the church in Ephesus, Paul said he had "not shunned to declare unto . . . [them] all the counsel of God. Take heed therefore unto yourselves," he added, "and to all the flock, over the which the Holy Ghost hath made you overseers, to feed the church of God, which he hath purchased with his own blood" (20:27, 28).

Paul expressed this thought repeatedly when writing to and when talking with leaders of the churches. He wrote to the Colossians with a message for Archippus, "Take heed to the ministry which thou hast received in the Lord, that thou fulfill it" (Colossians 4:17). He admonished Timothy to "endure hardness, as a good soldier," and not get entangled "with the affairs of this life" (2 Timothy 2:3, 4).

Paul confessed in terms of his own life that there was no time for resting upon one's laurels, no time for thinking one has it made in this spiritual warfare, acknowledging:

> Brethren, I count not myself to have apprehended: but this one thing I do, forgetting those things which are behind, and reaching forth unto those things which are before, I press toward the mark for the prize of the high calling of God in Christ Jesus. Let us therefore . . . be thus minded (Philippians 3:13-15).

Some labor in positions or under circumstances where it is necessary to earn money in secular or outside occupation. Scriptures do not condemn this. Paul himself was a tentmaker. There is, however, a difference between earning money in order to preach the gospel and forsaking the gospel in order to earn money. God's men keep the call and the ministry first. All else is secondary.

3. *The minister must not succumb to a life of luxury and ease.* A few years ago this pitfall was virtually nonexistent for the Spirit-filled, Pentecostal minister. Ministers today, however, often labor in the midst of plenty. They live in nice homes, drive fine automobiles, dress and eat sumptuously. The pitfall, of course, is not in the materialism itself, but in that waywardness of heart that makes a man think the accouterments of ministry are the essence of God's favor. It is possible for a man to become too comfortable, too relaxed, too much at ease with himself and his surroundings; and, amid such luxury, to cease hearing the still, small voice of God.

Jesus never implied that His call would be easy. He did not speak of luxury and flowery beds of ease: He *did* speak of the yoke, the plow and the Cross. Jesus did not call disciples to join Him in a lark. He asked men to volunteer as soldiers in a spiritual battle. "Blessed are ye," Jesus said, "when men shall revile you, and persecute you, and shall say all manner of evil against you falsely, for my sake. Rejoice, and be exceeding glad: for great is your reward in heaven: for so persecuted they the prophets which were before you" (Matthew 5:11, 12).

This theme is found throughout the New Testament. Timothy was told to "endure hardness, as a good soldier" (2 Timothy 2:3). Paul compared his sufferings for the sake of the Galatians to that of a woman travailing in birth (see Galatians 4:19). In Acts 15 the elders of Jerusalem referred to Paul, Barnabas, Judas and Silas as men who had 'hazarded their lives" for the sake of Jesus Christ (vv. 26, 27).

Had Paul been like some preachers today, he would never have responded to the Macedonian call. He would never have journeyed repeatedly across Asia Minor, and suffered cold, shipwreck, beatings and imprisonments. Rather, Paul would have settled down in one place and made himself comfortable. He would also have consigned himself to oblivion; we would know little if anything of the stalwart soldier who could say in the closing moments of his life "I have fought a good fight" (2 Timothy 4:7).

God still gives men the choice.

4. *The minister must avoid jealousy.* This monster seldom confronts a man straight on, or during the light of day. Jealousy stalks in evening shadows. Jealousy whis-

pers during the night. Jealousy accuses the brethren and exaggerates the slights. It turns one's eyes earthward, making him wallow in self-pity and blame God for his own second-rate performance.

There is absolutely nothing rational in jealousy. Yet men fall victim. For the most part, this happens when men compare themselves with others rather than with the Lord Jesus Christ. A man across town is praised, another is promoted, the former pastor is given the credit—reason argues that the other man's blessing does not change one's personal circumstance. In other words, it takes not one thing from a man to give his brother a nicer church. The first man still has whatever he had before, except for the jealousy Satan has planted in his heart. Unless cast out by the power of God, jealousy will ruin and destroy any man.

Solomon said, "Jealousy is the rage of a man" (Proverbs 6:34), and "cruel as the grave" (Song of Solomon 8:6).

Some actually feel jealousy is a back-door form of admiration, in that a man is never jealous of someone he does not admire. Jealousy may also stem from deep feelings of inadequacy, either known or unknown. Whatever the psychological explanation, jealousy is of the devil. It will inevitably reflect itself in a man's preaching. It is a spirit that will destroy a minister in today's world just as surely as it caused King Saul to lose his peace of mind, his kingdom, and his soul.

5. *The minister must not be frivolous.* There is not anything wrong with preachers laughing. Humor is excellent catharsis for the heart, and it would do some ministers good if they would not take every word and every incident too seriously; but the call of God and

the challenge of saving souls is not a frivolous matter. It is not something to consider lightly.

For the most part, frivolity among preachers is manifested through exaggeration or through lightness in the pulpit. For the praise of their peers or for the massaging of their own egos, preachers have been known to inflate their reports, to speak of revival and Sunday school attendance results which they never had, and even to recount true spiritual experiences with an emphasis on man rather than on the God of all miracles. Others stoop to telling off-color jokes, failing to realize that they deface the image of the ministry and that they could so weaken a young Christian's faith as to destroy a soul.

The rich young ruler would probably have followed Jesus part-time. He would have enjoyed the role of discipleship if it had not been too demanding and not too serious. Jesus loved the young man, but Jesus would not accept such a follower then, and He will not do so today.

When men and women face the big issues of life, when they confront crises, when they are ensnared in grief, when they despair of all hope—they turn to God's man. They do not wish to hear a joke, or to be confronted by someone who views their problems lightly. People want a man with heart, a man with love, a man with spiritual fervor and inner fiber who can wrestle with the prince of evil and bring an answer from the throne of God.

The ministry is serious business. Reports that circulate about a man, from family to family and from community to community, are the important ones.

Paul wrote to Titus, "In all things shewing thyself a pattern of good works: in doctrine shewing uncorruptness, gravity, sincerity, sound speech, that cannot be condemned; that he that is of the contrary part may be ashamed, having no evil thing to say of you" (Titus 2:7, 8).

The minister in today's world must have a good report, remembering that God keeps the true record.

6. *The minister must not commercialize his call.* Some men enter the ministry with an attitude that says they are all out for God and the Kingdom. Then, somewhere along the way, they shift to one that says, "The Kingdom is all right, but I want something for myself on the side." This is commercializing the gospel.

God calls all types of men into the ministry. Some are ordinary men made successful through the power of God's Spirit and God's wisdom in their lives. Others come to the ministry with highly obvious talents in business, music, education or communications. Satan never likes to lose any man from his ranks. He will always seek to corrupt and to lead the preacher away from the Cross. Obviously, one method for doing just this is to trick a man into trying to commercialize his ministry.

Elisha's servant Gehazi is a classic example (see 2 Kings 5:15-27). We have every reason to think Gehazi was a faithful servant until he saw the wealth of Naaman and decided there would be nothing wrong in receiving a little of all that silver. After Elisha refused Naaman's gifts, and after Elisha sent Naaman on his way back to Syria, Gehazi ran after Naaman and accepted silver and raiment in the name of Elisha.

Gehazi's act was one of fraud. He acted in the name of Elisha, not in his own name and not in accordance with his own needs or desires. Some preachers mistakenly think what they do is their business only. They think it is no concern of others. But it is! When one minister speaks or acts in the name of the church or in the name of Christ whom all ministers serve, then all ministers have a stake in his actions. When one man defiles the public image and commercializes the ministry for personal gain, then all members of the body suffer.

This explains the terrible judgment that came upon Gehazi. Elisha said to him, "Is it a time to receive money, and to receive garments, and oliveyards, and vineyards, and sheep, and oxen, and menservants, and maidservants?" (v. 26). Gehazi was therefore afflicted with Naaman's leprosy. He walked out of Elisha's presence with flesh as white as snow.

Satan makes his pitch with subtlety. He tells a minister it is for the family's sake, or that everyone else is doing it, or that the other man would do the same thing under these circumstances. The pit is thus camouflaged, and all too often good men are snared.

No man can divide his heart and remain a whole person. Jesus explicitly pointed out that man cannot serve both God and mammon. One cannot follow two masters. God's man is to seek first the kingdom of God. This is not a problem of our generation alone, although the temptation now may be more glaringly obvious. The New Testament church faced the same temptation. Writing to Timothy, Paul said a bishop should not be "greedy of filthy lucre" (1 Timothy 3:3), placing the man with this weakness alongside drunkards, strikers and brawlers. He repeated the statement in his letter to Titus (see 1:7).

The minister's proper attitude seems best expressed by the apostle Peter: "Feed the flock of God which is among you, taking the oversight thereof, not by constraint, but willingly; not for filthy lucre, but of a ready mind" (1 Peter 5:2).

Summary

What the minister is as a person, how he thinks and acts, where he places his emphases, his list of priorities—these are elements that combine to determine a man's success as a minister. These are not the only elements—not even the most important elements, perhaps, for we have mentioned previously the eternal nature of the Word and the miraculous working of the Holy Spirit—but they are elements that revolve around the minister's free-moral agency. In this sense, they are worthy of close attention.

God's man must take the call seriously. He must view himself properly, worthless without grace but valuable as God's chosen instrument.

"I keep under my body," Paul said, "and bring it into subjection: lest that by any means, when I have preached to others, I myself should be a castaway" (1 Corinthians 9:27).

The Pulpit and Pentecostal Preaching

Introduction

In our culture, most people respect the pulpit. For many, it may be something of a superstitious respect, as seen with the lay speaker who does not object to standing before the congregation but refuses to position himself behind the sacred desk; but it is respect just the same. Every minister must know that such respect exists and must act accordingly.

For our purposes here, of course, we are defining pulpit as something more than the podium itself. The pulpit is that point in both time and space where the man of God stands to read and preach the unsearchable riches of God. He may stand in a cathedral of glass, he may be on a street corner, or in a prison chapel; it does not matter. When the man of God stands up in the name of the risen Christ and when he opens his mouth to speak the Word of Almighty God, that place becomes the pulpit and, as such, it becomes a sacred and respected place both speaker and listener should honor.

The object of this chapter will be to look at how the man of God performs in the pulpit. First, though, we will examine the divine view of what man is in the pulpit, and then the human view of what man is in the pulpit.

God's View of Man in the Pulpit

Once again, we face the awesome realization that God has chosen to work through men in the carrying forth of His eternal plan of redemption. The Scriptures speak explicitly about how God views the role of the minister. Not only is this seen throughout the Old Testament, in the lives of priests, prophets, judges and rulers, it is also clearly set forth in New Testament language and in examples of apostles and missionaries who went forth with the gospel.

1. *Preachers are ordained of God.* Theirs is not a work of human origin, not a program of human design, or of human initiative. "Ye have not chosen me, but I have chosen you," Jesus said to the disciples, "and ordained you, that ye should go and bring forth fruit, and that your fruit should remain: that whatsoever ye shall ask of the Father in my name, he may give it you" (John 15:16).

Moses, Samuel, John the Baptist—these were men called and touched of God before their births. Paul was careful to point out that his life prior to his meeting Christ shaped and equipped him for the latter task. This is a truth to which every called minister can attest. God's providence is such that He never wastes those early years of a man's life; rather, He uses them to mold and shape men for His glory in special and miraculous ways.

God ordains ministers first. The church then sanctions that divine call and commission.

2. *Preachers are ministers of Christ.* Jesus sent His disciples forth to speak and act in His name—to cast out devils, heal the sick and preach the gospel. He gave the disciples power to bless those who heard and responded, and He clearly indicated that woe and judgment would rest upon those who refused to hear (Mark 6:11).

Paul referred to himself as "an apostle, (not of men, neither by man, but by Jesus Christ, and God the Father, who raised him from the dead)" (Galatians 1:1). Recounting his personal testimony before King Agrippa, Paul told how he met Christ on the road to Damascus. Jesus said to Paul,

> Rise, and stand upon thy feet: for I have appeared unto thee for this purpose, to make thee a minister and a witness both of these things which thou hast seen, and of those things in the which I will appear unto thee; Delivering thee from the people, and from the Gentiles, unto whom now I send thee (Acts 26:16, 17).

Paul's life illustrates how it is possible for a man to be ordained of God, called of God, commissioned of God, and yet have problems of acceptance with some brethren. Those early believers were not anxious to welcome the same Saul who had persecuted them and who had brought great harm and suffering to the

Christian fellowship. Theirs was a natural, human reticence; and it can be assumed, just as naturally, that Paul faced the temptation to ignore the Jerusalem elders and continue doing his own thing. That is not what happened. Paul persisted in his efforts to establish communication and fellowship with the brethren in Jerusalem, and God continued to confirm Paul's apostleship through miracles and the winning of souls. Eventually, the breach was healed and the church marched forward in unity.

3. *Preachers are stewards of God.* It should be understood that our concept of a steward differs greatly from that of New Testament times. We think of the steward as someone who manages household affairs or who sees to the comfort of passengers on a plane or ship. These individuals today are viewed more or less as high-priced servants. In the days of Christ, stewards represented much more. Jesus gave a number of parables relative to stewards, all clearly indicating the steward's major role in social and economic life. Stewards were the chief overseers, the supervisors, the absolute and total managers of massive estates. When we think of ourselves as stewards of God, as Paul wrote to Titus, it is much more accurate to remember Joseph's position as steward in the employ of Pharaoh.

Ministers are charged with the responsibility of managing God's affairs on earth. This means the minister must be "blameless . . . not self-willed, not soon angry, not given to wine, no striker, not given to filthy lucre; But a lover of hospitality, a lover of good men, sober, just, holy, temperate; Holding fast the faithful word as he hath been taught, that he may be able by sound doctrine both to exhort and to convince the gainsayers" (Titus 1:7-9).

Peter said it beautifully:

> As every man hath received the gift, even so minister the same one to another, as good stewards of the manifold grace of God. If any man speak, let him speak as the oracles of God; if any man minister, let him do it as of the ability which God giveth: that God in all things may be glorified through Jesus Christ, to whom be praise and dominion for ever and ever. Amen (1 Peter 4:10, 11).

4. *Preachers are ambassadors of God.* Political ambassadors are powerful men. They travel with special privilege. They enjoy unusual immunities. They speak with the power and the authority of the governments they represent. To insult an ambassador is to insult his government. Ambassadors usually live in protected embassies which are the property of their governments. Embassies are, for the most part, too sacred and too respected to touch.

Paul was keenly aware of the privileges of citizenship in the Roman Empire—he appealed to his own citizenship in order to have his trial transferred to Rome—and he surely understood as well what it was like to be a special envoy of Caesar. This is what Paul meant when he noted in his letter to the Corinthians that we are "ambassadors for Christ" (2 Corinthians 5:20). We speak for Christ. We speak in Christ's name and with His authority. We have His seal upon our heart and His Spirit within us. Back of us, we have the power and authority of heaven. We are, through Him, more than a match for Satan and the powers of evil.

5. *Preachers are ministers of reconciliation.* We are not ambassadors engaged in deceit. We are not seeking to sow discord or to create disorder in the world. Ours is not a task to be done in darkness, not an assignment to be carried out clandestinely in the back halls of power; but it is a noble and beautiful commission. Ours is the ministry of reconciliation.

We are ministers of light, bearers of truth, heralds of good news to all men everywhere. We are peace-loving, law-abiding, kind, merciful and friendly neighbors.

As ministers, we reconcile parents with children, citizens with government officials, neighbors with neighbors, husbands with wives. Our ministry of reconciliation spans the gamut of human relationships, but it starts and finds its perfect expression in the reconciling of man with God. All other efforts draw small circles, but the ministry of God's ambassadors embraces the whole human experience, proclaiming for all that God is in Christ reconciling the world unto Himself. Such is the good news of the gospel. Such is the important news of the minister.

This is how God sees the preacher, how God views a man when he steps into the pulpit. What an awesome responsibility rests upon one who dares speak according to what "thus saith the Lord."

The Human View of Man in the Pulpit

Understandably, people do not always see the minister as God sees him and as the Scriptures describe him. This is caused in part by the fact that human eyes are imperfect receptors, and in part by the fact that the minister does not always live up to, and perform according to, the high standard God desires. Nevertheless, people have some definite perceptions of ministers. There are some outward and human indications of what a preacher is and by which people tend to evaluate and judge him. We now propose to examine some of these human elements.

1. *People see the preacher in terms of his burden for the ministry and his love for people.* The preacher must truly care or he is marked for failure. Love cannot be imitated. Love has no substitute. It may be possible for some men to fool a few people part of the time, but they will not do so for long. True colors will show. People know—they sense it—when they are truly loved.

More than any other, it is this truth that explains how some men poorly equipped otherwise can yet be overwhelmingly successful in the ministry. They have few advantages in terms of education, they are not polished, not masters of oratorical skills; yet they inspire in their parishioners a loyalty and a devotion which cannot be disputed. Such men discover Paul's "more excellent way" (1 Corinthians 12:31).

Omitting the nonessentials, refusing to bog themselves down with things frivolous and unimportant, they concentrate on an affair of the heart. They give themselves to the Spirit, and to the mind of Christ. In short, they love people as they are and for what they are. They do so with such openness and sincerity that those who disagree with them in terms of a present issue will, at the same time, agree with them in spirit and follow along. "Now abideth faith, hope, charity, these three, but the greatest of these is charity" (13:13).

2. *People see the preacher in terms of his conversation.* The preacher is, first of all, a spokesman. While he does not

always claim to be speaking for God, he is nevertheless held accountable and judged on the basis of what he says. This is true of all Christians, but it seems especially applicable to the minister of the gospel. In such a busy world, it is not necessary that the man of God promise to be everything and do everything for everybody, but it is important that the preacher keeps the promises he makes. The preacher is not the only person on earth with a busy schedule. Church members and other professional people have their plans and schedules as well. Tardiness, failure to show up for appointments, negligence in terms of commitments—these characteristics are little foxes that spoil the vine in terms of relationships.

Obviously there is no place in the life of a minister for smut, for off-color jokes, or for puns which hint at a double meaning. Ministers have not only the right but the obligation to discuss all facets of human life— this includes the seamy side of life as well as the open and upright—but ministers must approach such subjects soberly and from a proper perspective. From the abundance of the heart the mouth speaketh. The man of God cannot afford to be labeled as having a dirty mind. Whether fair or not, whether correct or not, people judge the preacher to a great extent in accordance with his conversation.

Paul wrote to Timothy, "Be thou an example of the believers, in word, in conversation" (1 Timothy 4:12). Preachers should pray with the psalmist, "Set a watch, O Lord, before my mouth; keep the door of my lips" (Psalm 141:3).

3. *People see the preacher in terms of how he handles his personal life.* The man who preaches patience, thrift and

temperance should be a man who does not become easily angered, who does not stay in bed late every morning, and who does not eat himself into a state of obesity.
The man who emphasizes honesty and stewardship
should be one who pays his debts and is not stingy
with the church and God's kingdom.

Self-discipline does not come easily to any man or
woman. Most people have areas of self-discipline that
are more difficult than others, but the true shepherd
understands that he preaches by what he does as well
as by what he says, and he pays the price.

4. *People see the preacher in terms of how he relates to
his family, peers and other people.* It seems to be a law—
an unspoken law of human nature—that one cannot
respect those who do not respect others Even when we
are human enough to agree with the rumor or with the
negative assessment someone shares about another
individual, deep down we lose a little respect for the
person so speaking. So it is in terms of how members
view the preacher: if he does not show respect for his
family, his peers and his fellow laborers then a little
something dies and that minister no longer stands
quite so tall.

Let a minister speak angrily to his child in public,
and notice what happens. The public may agree that
the child needed to be reprimanded; they may understand that the situation demanded attention, but they
will know as well that the minister's anger showed
frustration and weakness rather than assurance and
strength. It is such knowledge, conscious or uncon-
scious, which brings the man of God down from his
perch and which may, with the accumulation of other
blotches, reduce him to a state of ineffectiveness.

"Do unto others as you would have them do unto you"—the rule applies to all and is a priority for those who propose to lead and to speak in the name of the Master.

5. *People see the preacher in terms of his denominational relationship.* People are not ignorant. Those who understand the gospel, and those who have the faintest concept of what the church is all about, know full well that Jesus promised to build His church, something greater and more magnificent than any individual. Most people take legitimate pride in being associated with an organization that spans generations and centuries, one that looks beyond the present and labors for tomorrow. They are far more willing to invest their time, their talent and their money in the broad goals of an organization than in the narrow limits of one man's life and ambition.

No man can cultivate faithfulness to himself while at the same time being faithless to his church superiors. If the preacher shows disrespect for the denomination he sows seeds of discord that will produce bitter fruit. When the harvest comes in, that man will be disappointed. Even when apparent success, or temporary success, accompanies the ministry of those who rebel and opt for so-called independence, it is this author's opinion that the work becomes as hay and stubble and will not survive (see 1 Corinthians 3:12, 13).

Who would wish to give his life to something that will die with the founder? Jesus solicits workers in an eternal project. Wise ministers protect and defend the denominational relationship. They value it for what it is and does, and they promote the same respect and consideration in their members. As the priests are; so are the people, says Hosea 4:4, 5.

With God, we are "workers together" (2 Corinthians 6:1).

6. *People see the preacher in terms of his relationship with the opposite sex.* This item deserves special mention because of its explosive nature. Here we deal with a matter so touchy that carelessness, not to mention sin, can destroy a man's effectiveness. Further complicating the matter for our day is the changing role of women and the new freedoms of a more promiscuous age.

Preachers minister to all people, rich and poor alike, male and female alike. In order to properly carry out his responsibilities, the preacher must be nondiscriminatory in his approach to people. Fact is, in most of our churches, female membership outnumbers male membership. Women teach most of the classes, perform most of the charitable duties, and raise most of the funds for expansion and ministry. No preacher can be successful unless and until he has a proper, well-developed, mature attitude toward the opposite sex.

Some ministers are chauvinistic and condescending toward women. They seek their support and their participation in the church's programs but fail to praise, to give proper credit, or to dignify the female contribution as of equal importance with the male. Other men are over-solicitous. They say to the women "Do it for me," rather than "Do it for God"; and they approach projects with such a maudlin attitude that they antagonize the men. Both approaches are beneath the dignity of God's ambassador.

Here are some suggestions:

• Give attention to your own marital relationship. Keep your marriage alive and working; and do not hesitate to let your people know that all is well.

- Treat all members with respect and dignity. Among other things, this means to respect confidences.

- Always view circumstances in their best, most positive light. Do not let the evil one pollute your thoughts with unfounded suspicions.

- Conduct your pastoral visits, your counseling sessions, and your social contacts in an open, professional, and upright manner, with an eye for how they are perceived by others.

- Be ultracautious when dealing with emotionally unstable people, and never try to help beyond that point for which you are professionally and spiritually prepared.

- See that your visits and counseling sessions center on spiritual rather than social notes.

- Pray often and strengthen yourself in the Word.

- Do everything possible to avoid gossip, but do not permit evil minds or wagging tongues to keep you from ministering to human needs.

How a Man Performs in the Pulpit

After all else is said and done, the man of God is first and foremost a preacher; therefore, he must be adept, he must have skill in the art of preaching. The supreme objective of preaching is to communicate the Word of God. Secondary goals are to inform, to teach, to challenge and to inspire. Men differ as to their skills, as to their methods, as to their chosen styles; but no man preaches successfully if he does not communicate.

Verbosity, difficult words, high-sounding phrases, technical language that is not required—these are smoke screens to be avoided. Say what you wish to say in straightforward, simple language. Explain it carefully. Speak it with conviction. Be bold in the power of God's Holy Spirit.

Not all men so act. Unfortunately, human and more carnal elements creep into sermons and some men have been guilty of profaning their pulpits. "The one preach Christ of contention, not sincerely, supposing to add affliction to my bonds: But the other of love, knowing that I am set for the defence of the gospel" (Philippians 1:16, 17).

Here are some negatives the man of God must avoid:

1. *The minister should never air his differences from the pulpit.* It would be great, of course, if there were no differences between the minister and his congregation, and certainly every effort should be made to keep them at a minimum; but, given the unglorified state in which we yet find ourselves, such differences continue to surface. They always will. Wise men learn how to place such irritants on the altar, how to exorcise them from their mind and heart even during study and preparation. Such men never take advantage of the pulpit.

Understandably, one deals here with a fine line. There may be times when a problem merits an answer from God's Word and the Holy Spirit bids the man of God to speak. It is even possible that the Word will cut sharply and keenly and the minister will be charged with malice when none exists. Such are risks all preachers run—risks which may be compounded in the preaching of that man who speaks extemporaneously and who depends on the leading of God's Spirit. One need not fear such risks, however, so long as the heart is kept pure and the motives sanctified. God's Spirit works on both sides of the pulpit, and people have a way of distinguishing between that which is of the Spirit and that which is of a bruised ego or of a crushed human spirit.

Ministers have a right to personal opinions, a right even to disagree with their members in terms of programs, politics, economics or social conditions; but they do not have the right to air such differences from behind the sacred desk and with the presumed sanction of almighty God.

2. *The minister should never reveal personal confidences.* This truth is so obvious that one would think, at first, that it is unnecessary to mention; but experience reveals otherwise. Some preachers would never think of going into the pulpit on Sunday and recounting a personal testimony about Sister Smith who is sitting in the congregation. They would not stand before a congregation and call names and places involved in a scandal. Nevertheless, these same men become guilty of dropping hints, of camouflaging illustrations and stories so thinly that certain people identify them. From that moment on, a crippled minister stands in the pulpit.

Other men tend to repeat what happened at a former pastorate, or they speak disparagingly of someone who once came to them with a problem. While this may make for good sermonizing or for keen illustrating, these men blunt their own effectiveness. It does not take an especially intelligent individual to conclude that if a preacher will tell about Sister Smith or Brother Johnson from where he last pastored, he will one day be referring to others also. What happens? People keep their personal problems to themselves. They fight their spiritual battles alone and the pastor is isolated and reduced to a mere functionary, rather than serving as a true shepherd.

3. *The minister should not discuss in public and from the pulpit matters which can be handled on a personal basis.* Frankly, some ministers are cowards. They have not the moral stamina or the inner fortitude to face a man or woman on a one-to-one basis and tell him or her what "thus saith the Lord." Rather, they do it from the pulpit. It is like the individual who tells someone something by writing a letter rather than facing the person head-on.

God calls men into the ministry. When an individual takes on a man's job, he should be prepared to stand up and act like a man. It is not easy. It is not pleasant. But it is effective. We know very little about the preaching ministry of Nathan; but we do know that, when he stood before King David and declared without blinking an eye, "Thou art the man," the message got results.

When the matter is personal opinion, or something totally private, there is even more reason why the minister should approach it face-to-face. The personal approach allows for defense and explanation. It permits the expressing of love and compassion. It preserves dignity, which none should needlessly destroy. It offers the best method for correction and, best of all, it is Scriptural.

4. *The minister should never display an unsympathetic attitude.* Such is not becoming to the spirit of Christ,

the ministry of reconciliation, or the compassion which should characterize the church. A belief in holiness does not give men a license to speak with callousness. Sin is a terrible thing. Sin is never to be condoned or sanctioned. But God loves sinners. Christ died for sinners. Thankfully, the patience of God far exceeds the patience of men. Speaking in the name of Christ, and as the mouthpiece of God, no person has a right to display in the pulpit a spirit or an attitude which is contrary to the New Testament; and, when someone does, the harm is broad and lasting.

Of all portraits one can draw of Jesus Christ from the Gospels, one that cannot be found is that of a mean and vindictive individual. Repeatedly, scriptures tell us, "Christ was moved with compassion."

5. *At the same time, the minister should not be timid, backward, or fearful.* Meekness is not weakness. Love is neither blind nor naive. God's man in the pulpit is not a tickler of ears and a soother of egos. The apostle Paul said, "For neither at any time used we flattering words, as ye know, nor a cloke of covetousness" (1 Thessalonians 2:5). He also said, "Do I seek to please men? for if I yet pleased men, I should not be the servant of Christ" (Galatians 1:10).

The minister stands in a sacred place. He speaks a glorious message. He is moved by a mighty anointing. And he offers a glorious gift. None is more significantly chosen, none more awesomely charged. The minister must be strong.

Summary

Few things are so beautiful as God's chosen and anointed man in the pulpit. The skeptic David Hume said of John Brown of Haddington, "Yonds the man for me. He preaches as if Jesus Christ were at his elbow."

So it should be.

Ian MacPherson accurately described the other side of preaching when he wrote: "There is forsooth a species of religious leadership which is simply the expression of uninhibited egoism. On the face of things it may appear marvelously effective. Things may get done. There may be a certain sleek efficiency in the running of the ecclesiastical machine. Round the pivotal personality there may cluster a coterie of doting admirers buzzing about like bees around a hive. But the whole thing is void of spiritual value. Never was the church meant to be organized round any human being however brilliant and magnetic. And the man who allows himself thus to be lionized in the house of God, not to speak of the man who deliberately courts it, is a ministerial Lucifer whose downfall is certain. True spiritual leadership is totally different."

Preparation for Pentecostal Preaching

Introduction

To the novice and the uninitiated, the act of preaching may seem a simple and uncomplicated performance. When one sits listening in the audience, taking in the phrases, slowly being carried along by the logic and clarity of a good sermon, it is easy to forget or to fail to appreciate the hours and the effort previously invested to make those thoughts conform to a plan designed to inspire the listener.

Good preaching is not simple. It does not just happen. It does not result from haphazard preparation: it is, rather, the result of a great many factors which climax at the moment of delivery. Good preaching comes only with sound, thorough, systematic preparation. It is possible, of course, for the experienced preacher to stand up and preach on the spur of the moment without a great deal of immediate preparation. Some men do this quite well. One should not conclude, however, that preparation is absent or that it is unnecessary, for such men to dip deeply into past studies and past experiences in life and pulpit.

This chapter will attempt to examine the full range of preparation for preaching. We will look first at that segment of preparation best termed as "formal," confining our definition to background education, specialized training such as Bible colleges and seminaries, and structured home study courses (which have become popular during the past few years and are available to almost every interested applicant). Next, we will examine the need for sound personal study habits and self-discipline. Finally, we will critique a systematic, step-by-step procedure for preparing to deliver a sermon.

As stated earlier, every step in ministerial preparation should be taken prayerfully and with full dependence on the Holy Spirit. The reader should understand this philosophy even though the approach here will deal with the human side of the equation, and make no attempt to emphasize the Holy Spirit's work in every section. Full attention will be given to the role of the Holy Spirit in subsequent chapters, notably chapter 8, "Pentecostal Preaching Is Prophetic."

Preparation in Terms of Education and Formal Training

All the education in the world, all the study and all the specialized training, will not produce a preacher unless the person is first called of God. Education and training may produce a skilled orator, turn out a brilliant businessman or manager, and qualify one to counsel and assist people psychologically with their troubles and their hang-ups; but such will never make a preacher. Preachers are called of God. They are commissioned and ordained of God to do a divine work through the sharing of a divine message. Quite obviously then, in accordance with this definition, preachers are something special.

Being called of God, being special in terms of God's providence, and being commissioned and entrusted with so serious a responsibility, it naturally follows that the man of God should take his calling seriously and should give himself totally to the task. In other words, sincere men always commit themselves to giving God their best. A man's best may not always include formal education. Circumstances, responsibility, age and many other factors make it impractical, if not impossible, for some men to prepare themselves formally for the Christian ministry. Every man's preparation, however, will include a giving of the total self, without reservation, and a willingness to study, to read and to learn how best to promote God's kingdom on earth. This willingness to give one's best will certainly require those who have opportunity for formal training to walk that path tenaciously, regardless of hardship or expense.

It would appear that some men seek formal education for carnal reasons. Other men rationalize. They have not the self-discipline, the fortitude or the courage to pursue a consistent course of study—although God would surely help them if they believed in miracles half so much as they often proclaim—and they cover their weakness by condemning those who honestly seek knowledge through formal study.

Each man should pursue knowledge and education in accordance with his personal opportunities and in relation to his personal goals, his calling and his other responsibilities. The man who feels God would have him serve as a missionary surely ought to prepare himself for life on a mission field. He who feels called to a specialized ministry such as counseling, education or rehabilitation will certainly need to prepare accordingly. For the young man especially, this matter is of serious consequence. It presents a dilemma with which every man should wrestle early and long, and over which he should pray sincerely. Once the decision is seriously and honestly made, then a man should live at peace with himself and without bitterness

Some ministers do not have opportunity to go to college. They enter the ministry late in life or after they have assumed family responsibilities. Sometimes they do not have the financial resources for such study. This does not, however, excuse any man from the serious task of learning all he can about the Word of God and about the people to whom he ministers.

Some men give themselves diligently to personal home study. They allot a certain number of hours for study each week. They learn the art of study from other men in the ministry or through reading widely. They slowly but surely acquire a store of knowledge that equips them admirably to serve the pulpit.

Of more consequence than anything said thus far is the fact that every minister must understand that the ministry demands a lifelong commitment to study and research. There never is a time—there will never come a time—when the successful preacher can cease reading and studying. Life itself is a matter of education. Of all people, the minister especially must continually probe and search for those truths to help others successfully negotiate the rocky paths.

Preparation in Terms of Self-Discipline and Personal Study

Being self-employed, the minister bears most of the responsibility for scheduling his time and study habits. He has no clock to punch, no specific hours to keep, and no boss looking over his shoulder. Nevertheless, every minister eventually faces the moment of accounting, and he will pay for neglect just as surely as a man in any other occupation. Preaching the gospel is not a performance of one hour. It is the revelation of a lifetime, the outflow of an infilling. In no other profession is the life of a man so vitally important to the success of his work.

Woodrow Wilson's father is said to have remarked, "A minister must be something before he can do anything." Always the preacher must speak of things he has tasted and handled of the Word of Life. He must partake before he can share. It is this personal drinking of spiritual water that makes up much of what is referred to here as preparation for preaching.

Study furnishes material for a sermon, but only prayer sanctifies it. Study stores facts and ideas in the mind, but prayer infuses a man's thoughts with divine influence. "Give attendance to reading," Paul told Timothy (1 Timothy 4:13); and it seems obvious that Paul continued to study till the end of his life, for he made this statement as he was preparing for death in a Roman prison.

Unfortunately for the minister, our culture's concept of work does not, for the most part, give value to contemplation or the process of creative thought. A minister sees this attitude displayed by members of his family, and, if he is not careful, he will come to share it.

For example, the man of God may be in his study thinking, praying, meditating and studying the Word. The phone rings and he learns that a member is in the hospital. How is the minister to react? Most ministers feel pressured to abandon the study, or the prayer closet, and go immediately to the member's bedside.

In an emergency, of course, there would be no alternative. But what happens to the minister who always feels this pressure? What becomes of the man who never has time alone? What does the future hold for the man who can never discipline himself to stay with the quiet moments, thus refurbishing his own soul?

The problem, basically, is a matter of priority. Ministers share the blame in that they permit themselves to be tricked into emphasizing certain duties to the exclusion of others. Deep down they feel it is more important to get out there and do something than to pray and study in order to be something. This may be most unfortunate.

Also, this may hint at leanness of soul and a spiritual condition that merits attention. J.H. Jowett stated, "We are not always doing the most business when we seem to be the most busy." John Calvin exposed his soul when he asked, "What deep-seated malice against God is this that I will do anything and everything but go to Him and remain in secret prayer."

Somehow one gets the feeling that Satan would prefer the preacher to occupy himself with almost any activity other than preparation, so long as he enters the pulpit empty rather than on fire with a relevant message.

Ours is the busiest society in history. Most people are compulsively busy, competitive and driven by a desire to outrun and outdo the other person. Such a concept can filter into the minister's thinking as well. It can sidetrack him from personal devotions and immersion in the Word, activity absolutely required if a man is to preach. The disciplined man will learn somehow to control his time. He will allot time for study, time for prayer, time for sermon preparation, time for visitation and time for those other duties.

He will learn to keep this schedule, and, in the keeping of it, he will guard his own soul and remain a preacher with a message, rather than a preacher with just a sermon when he walks into the pulpit.

Ministers can always be on the run, but wise men discipline their hours and bend them to God's will and purpose. Much of today's pressure may be caused from lack of discipline rather than from overwork. God would have His servants be balanced in their activities.

In terms of scheduling and making wise use of time, note the following suggestions:

1. Make sure nothing interferes with your private devotions. This is so vital that, if necessary, the preacher must arise early or stay up late.

2. Strip programs of nonessentials and learn to delegate responsibility.

3. Accept once and for all that study and prayer are priority items, not just time-fillers, and never feel guilty for investing in them.

4. Learn to live with incompletion and be at peace with yourself. Tomorrow is another day, another moment, another opportunity. Whatever you get done, there will always be more to do. God expects only what you are capable of doing. Leave the balance to Him.

5. Schedule your leisure time and your family activities with the same precision and the same faithfulness. Family responsibility is a priority and every minister

needs some time away from the daily grind. At least 10 times in the New Testament, Jesus mentioned retiring from the crowd. The Creation story itself lets us know every man needs a rest. For the preacher, weekends are not rest periods. He must find his leisure during the week and he must use it intelligently.

Preachers, too, are creatures of habit. Good habits assist tremendously when it comes to discipline. Periodically it is well for every minister to examine his life, perhaps to chart precisely how he divides his time. Such can be an interesting experience. Without examination, a man can find himself living in the wrong atmosphere. Like a mountaineer who has lived so long at high altitudes that he ceases to notice the beauty of the mountains, the preacher can come to where he is no longer conscious of his own weaknesses or failures.

At this point, fasting seems most advantageous to the man of God. Fasting disciplines the flesh. It makes things earthly and physical subservient to things heavenly and spiritual. Of course, no type of personal abuse or fleshly denial should be viewed as a currency with which to purchase some specific blessing from God, as some men have seemed to claim. Rather, fasting is one method, along with prayer, which permits a burdened man to draw nigh to God and tune his soul with the Almighty.

Jesus fasted. Old Testament prophets fasted. The New Testament disciples fasted. The apostle Paul gave himself often to this practice (see 2 Corinthians 11:27). In accordance with the leading of God's Holy Spirit, the Pentecostal preacher may on occasion declare a fast for his congregation. Also, the sincere man of God will certainly give himself to periods of fasting. It will be a vital part of his schedule. Spiritually burdened men hide themselves away and deny themselves in their search for God's will. Fasting is a must for Pentecostal preaching: it entreats God's presence, it sensitizes the soul, and it prepares the preacher to follow the direction of the Spirit. Take heed to yourself. Examine yourself occasionally in the light of the Word and with the aid of God's Holy Spirit. It is amazing what one can discover.

Preparation in Terms of a Single Person

There is quite a difference between a sermon and a message. One can learn how to build a sermon through a course in homiletics, but a man must go to God for a message. Giving birth to a message is not a light and chaffy matter. It costs a man something. It is spiritual travail.

Before ever daring to enter the pulpit, the minister must prepare himself to preach. Andrew Bonar once confessed in his diary what is so often the case with preachers on Sunday morning: "I was like one seeking his entrance into the holy place and fellowship of God, not like one coming out from communion to speak to others."

The pulpit is not the place for the minister to search for and find God, it is the place where the man who has been with God now speaks to others. Thorough preparation in terms of materials will come to naught if the minister has not seen the face of God. Of Phillips Brooks it was said that, before entering the pulpit, "he appeared like one burdened with a message from God."

These facts being understood, let us look more closely at the process of study itself. What the minister must do in order to preach has something in common with farming. First, he must garner, or gather, his materials: look for ideas, principles, truths applicable to the people he will address. Second, he must winnow, or discriminate: throw out the superfluous, the impractical—that which will take time but will not contribute significantly. Third, he must store, or retain (in his memory or through notes), those ideas and thoughts he will later speak white-hot to the people.

It should be reiterated that one should never seek to study without calling upon, and depending upon, the aid of God's Holy Spirit. One needs the Spirit for inspiration and to make the Word alive. One also needs the Spirit in order to rightly divide the Word.

The minister must have a broad understanding of the Bible. He should be saturated with the Bible's message, from Genesis to Revelation. He ought not ever give undue prominence to one portion: not because there is anything untrue or unimportant in the Bible, but because the Bible is God's continuing revelation of Himself to man. It is not to be dissected and studied in bits and pieces. The minister must preach the whole Bible, rightly divided. Some men concentrate on single passages, or off-beat themes, without considering other portions of Scripture. They think they have found a diamond when, in truth, they have been dazzled by a piece of glass.

God's Word is a holy place wherein the minister searches, not unlike the Holy of Holies in the Tabernacle. The minister must remember that the Word contains instruments for doing all that is needed in the spiritual lives of people. In the sanctuary of old, one could find the balances, but one could also find the sacrificial knife. So it is with the Word, and so it behooves the preacher to be led of God's Spirit. Those who weigh when God's Spirit bids use the knife and those who use the knife when the Spirit says to weigh are equally out of step; both will come to an ineffective conclusion. Paul wrote to the church at Colosse, "Let the word of Christ dwell in you richly in all wisdom" (3:16).

Richard Warren, in his book *Twelve Dynamic Bible Study Methods,* suggests in his introduction that every serious student of the Bible should . . .

1. Schedule a time for serious Bible study, preferably a time block of at least one hour
2. Keep a notebook
3. Get the right tools.

The minister may think it difficult to invest in a good, basic library—and it may be difficult in terms of finance—but certain tools are absolutely necessary. A minister can no more afford to do without proper tools than a carpenter can afford to work without hammer and saw. A basic library will vary somewhat, according to a man's special interests, but here are some suggestions . . .

- A study Bible
- An exhaustive concordance
- A Bible dictionary
- A topical Bible
- A Bible handbook
- A commentary
- A Bible encyclopedia
- A set of word studies
- Individual book commentaries
- A Bible atlas
- Old and New Testament surveys
- Other books of your own special interest.

Once the minister has a basic library, then he should acquaint himself with various Bible study methods. It is not likely that a man will use the same method of study all the time, even though most people eventually concentrate on a favorite method or two.

Avoid becoming a text hunter. Men who merely look for a special passage or a catchy phrase seldom are remembered for their effective preaching. While one may on occasion look at the sermon outlines of the pulpit masters, one should outline and build his own sermons, using those of other men only for comparative purposes or for seed thoughts.

This is not to suggest that a man ought never to repeat the great themes and subjects of the Bible. Certain themes, such as repentance, the new birth, holiness, the Resurrection, adoption, eternal life, and so forth deserve repetition on a regular basis, even though the Scripture texts used, and the point from which the sermon is launched, may vary. What is true of great subjects and themes is equally true of great texts of the Bible. As Spurgeon said, "Some of the texts of the Bible will seem to track you down and demand your attention."

There are any number of Bible study methods a man may choose. Most of these have been known and practiced by ministers for years, with slight variations, but Richard Warren lists his 12 methods with great clarity.

1. *The Devotional Method.* Select a short portion of your Bible and prayerfully meditate on it till the Holy Spirit shows you a way to apply the truth to your life. Write out a personal application.

2. *The Chapter Summary Method.* Read a chapter of a Bible book through at least five times; then write down a summary of the central thoughts you find in it.

3. *The Character Quality Method.* Choose a character quality you would like to work on in your life and study what the Bible says about it.

4. *The Thematic Method.* Select a Bible theme to study. Think of three-to-five questions you'd like to have answered about that theme. Study all the references you can find on your theme and record the answers to your questions.

5. *The Biographical Method.* Select a Bible character and research all the verses about that person in order to study his or her life and characteristics. Make notes of attitudes, strengths and weaknesses. Apply what you learn to your own life.

6. *The Topical Method.* Collect and compare all the verses you can find on a particular topic. Organize your conclusions into an outline you can share with another person.

7. *The Word Study Method.* Study the important words of the Bible. Find out how many times a word occurs in Scripture and how it is used. Find out the original meaning of the word.

8. *The Book Background Method.* Study how history, geography, culture, science and politics affected what happened in Bible times. Use Bible reference books to increase your understanding of the Word.

9. *The Book Survey Method.* Survey an entire book of the Bible by reading it through several times to get a general overview of its contents. Study the background of the book and make notes on its contents.

10. *The Chapter Analysis Method.* Master the contents of a chapter in the Bible by taking an in-depth look at each verse in that chapter. Tear each verse apart word by word, observing every detail.

11. *The Book Synthesis Method*. Summarize the contents and main themes of a book of the Bible after you have read it through several times. Make an outline of the book. This method is done after you have used a Book Survey Method and the Chapter Analysis Method on every chapter of that book.

12. *The Verse-by-Verse Analysis Method*. Select one passage of Scripture and examine it in detail by asking questions, finding cross-references, and paraphrasing each verse. Record a possible application of each verse you study. (*Twelve Dynamic Bible Study Methods*, by Richard Warren, Victor Books. Used by permission.)

Obviously, the method of study will be determined by what you as a minister are trying to accomplish. For some five decades, Dr. R. Hollis Gause influenced the theology and the preaching of the Church of God through his association with Lee College and the School of Theology. He always suggested to a young minister that he first have a good, basic understanding of the Bible in general, that he choose an area of study or a broad subject in which he wished to specialize, such as theology or prophecy; and, finally, that he choose one book of the Bible and determine to be an authority in terms of that book.

What Dr. Gause was noting is that no man can exhaust the Bible. No man can be a specialist and a total authority on every book and every passage of the Bible. Each man can, however, become something of an authority on a particular area of interest, and a man should give himself to that end. Such a goal makes for an exciting adventure in study and becomes tremendously satisfying from a personal perspective.

Summary

There seems to be too much fad preaching today, too much situation preaching, too much experience preaching; but not enough preaching of the Word.

There is a tendency among preachers to shirk the Word and to preach to please. Some men preach more in terms of what people want, or seem to enjoy, than in terms of what people need. But preaching is not preaching unless it is based on the Word. When a man stands before a congregation, he should see in their faces and attitudes, "Sirs, we would see Jesus."

Paul's first sermon declaration was Jesus Christ. The man of God today must not only preach the Word but he must preach the Word in such manner as to reveal the person and the Lordship of Jesus Christ. Illustrations and personal stories are fine and interesting—they attract attention and are excellent tools for driving home a practical application of truth—but they ought never be an end in themselves. Unfortunately, some preachers get more response out of recounting some occurrence than they get from the sermon itself. Such a fact cannot but reflect either on the substance of the sermon or upon the spiritual condition of the congregation: neither of which is complimentary.

Humor can, on occasion, be injected into a sermon. However, a joke may easily kill the conviction and render the message ineffective. The minister's task is to preach the Word! Be instant in season and out of season. Always preach the Word.

In order to preach, the minister must study. The minister must prepare himself to preach the Word: this preparation begins early in life (at least it begins immediately upon his receiving the call) and continues in various forms all the days of his life. Preparation involves many facets, but it is indispensable.

Those who do not study have no right to call upon God to make up the deficits of their idleness. That man who walks into the pulpit empty and dry will perform accordingly, although he may on occasion, or for a brief period of time, hide his weakness behind sound and fury.

Some men sing . . . or weep . . . or ask that the people rededicate themselves . . . or request a new appointment. . . . But God says to preach the Word.

And that demands preparation.

6

Pentecostal Preaching Is Precise

Introduction

The word *precision* means "exactness; relevance; the degree of refinement with which a certain operation is carried out." This may not be a term ordinarily applied to Pentecostal preaching, especially the reference to refinement, but the word points to something that needs to be said. Too much preaching today is pointless, without specific and concrete objective.

No preacher should enter the pulpit just to perform, to merely go through the motions of preaching. He should step forth with a goal in mind. He should know where he wishes to go, what he wishes to accomplish, and how he proposes to do it. Otherwise, preaching remains too much a hit-or-miss proposition and pulpit results remain less than what God demands and the congregation needs.

Some preachers are like a few school teachers I have known. They have a few key sermon outlines.

They have slumped into a habit of doing things a certain way, according to certain procedures, and they resent being forced to change. Just as teachers adjust to and get acquainted with a curriculum, so some preachers become routinely oriented to the comfort of their own ways.

God is not so limited. The Holy Spirit breathes fresh inspiration upon those willing to listen, and the Bible has new truths for the minister willing to discover and to share.

To carry the illustration one step further, some preachers pride themselves on their years of experience. They refer to 10 years' experience in the ministry, 20 years' experience, or 30; but, the truth is, they have one year's experience repeated 30 times. Like teachers, they think of themselves as tenured, having arrived at a special status by virtue of seniority alone, and they function perfunctorily. Such men are so passionless, so dry, so unmoved themselves that their preaching neither cuts nor burns.

But routine operation and pseudo-professionalism has no place in Pentecostal preaching. God's men have not the time for dealing in unfelt truths. Rather, they must give heed to Paul's admonition to "walk worthy of the vocation wherewith . . . [they] are called" (Ephesians 4:1).

It is great to live in a day when information is readily available. Nevertheless, easy access to others' ideas and thoughts may cause ministers to become lazy, mere hunters of texts and catchy phrases rather than anointed prophets of God. One ought not forget that study furnishes a man with materials, prayer sanctifies those ideas and concepts, but God gives the message. Real preaching is the cream of one's meditation, warmed by the Holy Spirit, and made to glow in a man's heart.

Invariably, this process makes it necessary that the true shepherd establish certain spiritual goals for himself and for his congregation. Once these goals are fixed and understood, preaching aims toward leading men and women in that direction. Within this context at least, ministers ought to preach with precision.

Knowing Your Audience

To preach well, the man of God must first know and understand his audience. It is true, of course, that certain issues and certain principles are common to all men. These are fair and fit subjects on which to preach. Such preaching may at times be rated good, it may produce some results; but it will not be great preaching until and unless it aims at the needs and spiritual concerns of the audience.

God's man must be a student of human nature. He must see people truly, noting the pain in their eyes, the shadows on their faces, the subtle and unspoken questions that register concern when he shakes a hand or brings up a subject. A minister is not wasting time when he visits in a member's home. He is not being distracted from his real task when he sits for a moment of fellowship over coffee or tea. He can well afford the few moments, even the hours, necessary to learn about families, children, financial difficulties, sicknesses, and personal battles. It will be this knowledge, this background, from which he will draw inspiration to pray and to search the Word. Also, upon these vital concerns he will lay the promises of God and call to bear the comfort of God's Holy Spirit from the pulpit.

Preaching with precision—truly great preaching—includes knowing and understanding the audience.

When a man has pastored the same congregation for a number of years, he may at times feel repetitious, or he may struggle for something fresh and vital to say. Men have said to me, "I need a new and fresh challenge." While this may be true on occasion, it is not of itself reason enough for changing pastorates. A man who knows his people, who understands them—and, at the same time, a pastor who is known and understood by his people—will often accomplish more with fewer words. Such a preacher learns to aim more precisely. He builds this week, or during this sermon, on all the precepts and principles he has laid down previously, and, for the most part, he will produce more spiritual fruit.

Experience bears this out. Men who have remained long in the same pastorate speak of the ebb and flow of spiritual tide. They refer to times of difficulty and spiritual drought, noting that refreshing rains soon follow. Not only is it true historically that some of the greatest preachers stayed long with the same congregation but now, even among Pentecostals, most of the more productive men are long-term pastors.

One thing is certain: being acquainted with people, knowing and understanding them, should in no wise be viewed as a hindrance to effective and precise preaching. Such must be listed on the positive side of the preaching ledger.

ESTABLISHING YOUR GOALS

All preachers have some goals, certain things they wish to accomplish with their lives and ministries. What is referred to here is more narrowly defined than that. It is important that the minister be aware of definite, definable preaching goals—goals that relate to the present challenge of his work, as opposed to the Great Commission at large, and goals into which he can set his teeth and evaluate preaching effectiveness.

Long-Range Preaching Goals

Preachers do themselves and their congregations a disservice when they fragment their preaching, when they make no attempt to connect subjects or to make sense out of the general direction the sermons are taking. This is not to imply that a minister should select 52 related subjects and then systematically enlarge upon them each Sunday morning—nor should such planning be condemned if it is done prayerfully and with allowance for adjustment—but every minister should establish long-range spiritual goals for his people. He should prayerfully choose subjects and Scriptural passages that further these goals. And he should evaluate the effectiveness of his preaching in terms of spiritual impact upon his listeners.

Long-range preaching goals should include the following:

1. *A congregation knowledgeable in the facts of the Word.* It is here where preaching begins. Ministers must teach the Word, the facts of the Word. One must do so first because not everyone goes to Sunday school, not everyone listens when they go, and not every subject is covered in the curriculum used. Such teaching may not be the primary thrust of one's preaching—it may be but a subtle thought woven in or an introductory sideline—but keep in mind that with time and persistence every good minister will add to his congregation's Biblical store of knowledge.

2. *A congregation knowledgeable in the application of the Word to its personal needs.* Application is the heart of preaching. Here the minister translates what happened to the psalmist into what can happen in the life of the listener. Historical events become prisms that focus brightly on the present. Certainly God spoke; God still speaks. God moved; God still moves. Wise pastors rejoice and discover new inspiration when they observe their members maturing and learning to apply the Word to their daily living.

3. *A congregation adept in using the Word for spiritual defense and strength.* The Word of God is "the sword of the Spirit" (Ephesians 6:17). The minister must wield the sword and teach his listeners to do so as well. Otherwise, they remain children. Sermons should be full of Word nuggets, for these are like sword thrusts, sharp and cutting: they are also weapons the listener can use on Satan. "He gave some, apostles; and some, prophets; and some, evangelists; and some, pastors and teachers" (4:11).

4. *A congregation equipped to minister the Word to others at their point of need.* Here it is that men sometimes fail, being content to entertain, to inspire, to make people feel better rather than to tackle the more difficult task of equipping them to go forth in power. Once it was said of Pentecostals, "Every one of them is a preacher." No matter how well the preacher ministers to the needs of his listeners, no matter how large the congregation, his goals are severely limited unless he trains others to go forth and witness.

5. *A congregation with a well-balanced spiritual diet.* Some who attend church are spiritually malnourished. They are anemic, their spiritual deficiency obvious.

They lack Word vitamins and Biblical minerals necessary for strength and vitality. Unless these people have a change of diet, they will die. Ministers must note this sickness. They must diagnose correctly and must serve a well-balanced meal.

Is it not odd, this human tendency to eat overlong and overmuch on what is not healthful? Paul noted in his letter to Timothy that the Word is a versatile and potent prescription (2 Timothy 3:16).

• People need doctrine. They need deep truths, systematic truths, great truths, even familiar truths. People need to be reminded of repentance, justification, regeneration, the new birth, sanctification, holiness, the baptism with the Holy Ghost, spiritual gifts, healing, judgment, stewardship, love, the Resurrection, and the Second Coming. They need doctrine, without which they will go astray and walk blindly into the devil's snares.

• People need reproof. Evil is to be exposed. Sin is to be condemned. Unrighteousness is to be so named and those who are involved must be reproved. While not a pleasant task, this too is the duty, the charge, the divine obligation of the preacher. One must swing hard and with precision. One must do so in love, aiming first at the restoration of the person in error; but one may, on occasion, have to publicly rebuke (see 1 Timothy 5:20) and cast out those who would destroy the flock (see 1 Corinthians 5:13). Whatever the occasion demands, the preacher is charged to minister, and God's Word is the instrument. No congregation is spiritually healthy if the element of reproof is missing from a man's sermons. It is the Word that rebukes; and, when it is preached in its fullness, this end will be accomplished (see 2 Timothy 3:16).

• People need correction. By nature some men are better equipped than others to discipline or to reprove; they are less adept at correcting. A man or woman may be publicly or instantly reproved; they may require months, and repeated efforts, for correction. Nevertheless, God's Word is profitable for correction. If the minister keeps searching for the right passage, if he prays and continues to administer the healing balm, correction will also take place and that individual so near the precipice will be drawn slowly and lovingly back into a full and comfortable relationship with God. True shepherds take no pleasure in the failure of souls. They do not count spiritual scalps or gloat over souls lost or turned out of the church, no matter the reason. True shepherds intercede with tears and with compassion, they apply the Word with gentleness, and they take pleasure in wrongs corrected.

• People need instruction. Note how beautifully and how progressively the headings move. Church members no more deserve being rebuked when they have not been instructed than do children. No minister has a right to complain when his people fail to do certain things unless he has first instructed them in how to go about doing them. Instruction is part of the task, part of the responsibility. This means more than mere listing of a few steps. Instruction means ideas carefully and systematically arranged. It means ideas set forth simply and in understandable terms. It means repetition until the truths have been imbedded in the listener's consciousness, and it should also mean motivating the individual to follow the instructions. The Word is profitable for instruction (see 2 Timothy 3:16).

Proper spiritual diet must be a priority in the long-range planning of every preacher.

Short-Range Preaching Goals

When one prepares for the pulpit upon any specific occasion, using a single subject or theme, he should also have a goal in mind—an immediate goal, a goal for the present moment. The preacher may aim . . .

- to convert sinners
- to inspire saints
- to encourage
- to comfort
- to teach
- to instruct
- to reprove
- to correct
- to motivate
- to make aware
- to call for commitment
- to challenge
- to give thanks
- to lead in worship.

Obviously, this list could be expanded almost infinitely. However, some men forget. They enter the pulpit with little in mind other than what they call "having church." They go into their sermon with no more objective than to see how the people like this one. Such is not preaching: it is certainly not Pentecostal preaching! It is little more than an exercise in futility. God's men preach with an objective in mind. They aim at something. They sight in on a specific problem and keep firing away with precision until something happens.

Today's preacher needs to be adaptable. He needs to be willing to innovate, to reschedule himself and his plans. No man can preach with precision until he has his goals in mind.

CHOOSING YOUR INSTRUMENTS

When one refers to a physician or to a lawyer, one understands immediately that the tools of their respective trades consist of medicine and laws. It is equally obvious that the mechanic must have tools and the carpenter must have building materials.

While not so apparent, the instruments with which the preacher works are also vital to success. Men who preach with precision know and understand the tools available. They realize what choices are theirs and, perhaps most important, they understand that it is what a man does with the tools rather than the tools themselves that will determine the end result of preaching.

Sermons are normally categorized according to a few distinct types: *expository preaching*—the minister chooses a full chapter or rather lengthy passage of Scripture and comments on it in a systematic way; *preaching from a text*—a shorter passage of Scripture, usually one or two verses, containing ideas or thoughts from which the sermon develops; *theme preaching*—chosen from any number of passages and followed according to logical sequence; and *subject preaching*—picked from current events, from history, or from any other point of interest upon which the minister develops his own thoughts.

While these four types of sermons are most representative of preaching, in terms of homiletics, they do not exhaust the categories. Much preaching today is a combination of these various types rather than a display of pure form. Such seems especially true in terms of Pentecostal preaching. While a man may speak on a subject, say *courage*, he will probably introduce the subject with a text verse, then sprinkle his points with many other references to God's Word.

Ministers choose—at least they can choose—the type sermon which will best help them reach individual objectives. For example, the pastor concerned about increasing his congregation's knowledge of the Word may choose to use expository preaching for a period of time; but, if he wishes to preach on stewardship, he may opt for a theme or subject approach.

With these options in types of sermons, ministers also choose between various ways for delivering the message. Some men preach from a full manuscript, some from a thorough outline, some from a simple main-point outline, and yet others extemporaneously. While extemporaneous preaching may seem most desirable among Pentecostals, and while this may appear to be the form of preaching most effective, it should be noted that few men speak totally extemporaneously. They may speak without notes, they may move their thoughts forward with precision and apparently without guidance from an outline; but, except on rare occasions, such men follow a mental outline or else they draw from a vast store of experience that permits the charting of a logical course.

Young ministers should not feel intimidated because they do not have this background experience. Rather, they should study, pray, outline their thoughts and then enter the pulpit with both an objective in mind and a commitment to follow the Spirit of God.

No matter the type sermon, or the approach chosen, there are other keys vital to preaching with precision.

One purpose of preaching is to convince men and women of the truth. A preacher, thus, must present his argument in some sort of logical sequence. Like a lawyer, he must begin with a known or accepted truth. From that point of agreement, he must proceed to build with evidence toward a greater or more important conclusion.

Paul's sermon to the Greeks on Mars Hill is an excellent example (see Acts 17). Paul introduced his sermon by referring to one of the Athenians' statues dedicated "To the Unknown God."

"I wish to tell you about this God," Paul said. Then Paul proceeded to present his case for a supreme God, One who created heaven and earth. Such a God, Paul noted, cannot be made to dwell in temples erected by human hands. Nor does He need anything of human hands, since He is the Creator of all.

Can you see Paul's logic? From there he moved on to tell of Jesus Christ.

With his lawyer's background, Charles G. Finney was a great preacher through logical argument. Some Pentecostal preachers today are also effective because they present the Word in its own beautiful and logical format.

Ideas should be clear, set forth in precise language, easily understood. Some men seem to think their preaching is enhanced by a sprinkling of big words and complex phrases. Such only confuses the listener. One should never use a large word, when a simple one will convey the same thought; and, when complex theological terms are necessary, the wise preacher defines them carefully. For the preacher, few compliments are more beautiful than, "You make the Bible simple enough for a child to understand."

Human interest stories, anecdotes, poetic phrases, statistics, humor, parables—these may all be used on occasion to shed light on the minister's subject. They should be carefully chosen. However, one must be constantly on guard to see that they are kept in perspective, that they illuminate the subject rather than becoming an end in themselves. It is better never to tell a story than to tell one that takes the focus of attention from the subject.

We live in a visual age. Men and women have short attention spans. They are geared to 30-second commercials and fast-moving TV scripts. Whether for good or bad, this generation is time-conscious and will not stay long with the preacher whose thoughts circle and who repeats himself. Listeners demand movement. They must feel the sermon is going somewhere, that there is aim and purpose. In short, when the speaker's thoughts no longer progress, the listener's thoughts move on to something else, leaving the preacher to wonder what happened.

It is often said that truth is stranger than fiction. Of all people, preachers must be careful to establish the credibility of their remarks. They cannot afford to make people doubt their words, even if some "far-out," sensational story is the truth. Credibility between speaker and audience is necessary not only for convincing people, but also for getting them to listen in the first place.

Some men paint pictures with their words. Others drag listeners to a slow and painful "amen." Congregations resist pain, and people shy away from mental cruelty. Thus, unless a speaker's words are set forth in an interesting style, the listener usually permits his mind to wander.

Speak to people's needs, their hurts, their fears and their concerns, for men and women are interested in themselves. If the preacher's words center there, the congregation will be interested in what is said.

Unless words and ideas are exciting to the preacher, there is no way they will create much excitement on the part of a listener. Enthusiasm is necessary,

One should build his ideas on the Word. It is what "thus saith the Lord" that really matters. Men may take issue with the speaker's concepts and thoughts, but they cannot argue with the Word of God. Preaching must always be founded upon the Word.

Two men may stand before an audience and say the same thing. One will impress, the other will not. One will move people, the other will not. One will leave an impact, the other will not. To preach with precision, the man of God must phrase his words and statements in a positive manner. He must speak with simple, straightforward sentences. He should not permit his statements to drag out with subordinate clauses. Punch the words home. It is impact that really matters.

Impact will determine response, of course; and response will determine whether one is an effective or an ineffective communicator of the truths of God. It is not enough to speak, to get through the morning: one must motivate men and women to respond to the gospel.

I have heard men who were not at all polished, who were not at all educated or trained in the finer points of oratorical skill; but, when they concluded their message, when they lifted their hands in prayer, when they stood with tears streaming down their cheeks, when they invited men and women to Christ, something happened. A man can afford to do without some of these things mentioned, but no preacher can afford to do without response to the gospel.

These then are some of the instruments the man of God chooses and uses to make his message precise and effective. No one uses all of them all of the time. Many preachers use them without being conscious of what they are doing. However, there is one other vital statement to be made, without which one might think preaching is a purely mechanical process.

Warming Your Heart

Preaching is more than reciting a few facts and figures. It is more than speaking sentences and neatly phrased words. Preaching is, in it purest form and at its best, a miracle that blends a human instrument with the Holy Spirit's purpose and power. Some men discover this all too well when they quickly grab a sermon outline and rush into the pulpit thinking they can do again what they once did. How sad!

They speak only words, for God's Spirit and power is absent.

The man of God must warm his heart at the altar. He must pray through and feel deeply the truths he plans to give to others. When the heart is thus warmed, and when the minister can thus yield to the move of God's Spirit, he preaches. This is Pentecostal preaching; and, in this author's opinion, it is preaching at its best.

Summary

To preach with precision, the man of God must first know his audience. He must establish both long-range preaching goals and goals for the immediate sermon. He must choose instruments that will make a particular sermon most effective. Finally, he must warm his heart through prayer and then yield to the Spirit of God.

7

Pentecostal Preaching Is Productive

Introduction

When all else is said and done, a man's preaching will be judged on the basis of results. Some men will agree with this statement and, at the same time, judge preaching results by different criteria. The statement is true, nonetheless, and the results that matter are those calculated in heaven's script. A preacher's final witness is in heaven: "Behold, my witness is in heaven, and my record is on high" (Job 16:19).

The results of one's preaching are not always immediately visible, but every minister should work and evaluate himself first in terms of those overt (and sometimes covert) indications that God is, through His Word, producing miraculous changes in human lives. To do otherwise is contrary to that New Testament pattern of preaching that so transformed the world.

For this reason, a very practical heading has been chosen for this chapter. While understood that this author considers himself to be first an evangelist, therefore partial to preaching results that center around an altar of repentance, it should not be concluded that evangelistic results are the only benefits of preaching.

As noted earlier, preaching should take aim—it should center on an objective. One of the more glorious objectives of preaching is the winning of sinners to the Lord. Back of all else he does, no matter his other responsibilities and tasks, every minister comes eventually to his responsibility for preaching evangelistically. It is here our thinking will concentrate for the moment, for we are using the phrase "preaching productively" as being somewhat synonymous with "preaching evangelistically."

Evangelistic Preaching Parallels the New Testament Pattern

Paul wrote to Timothy, his son in the Lord, "Do the work of an evangelist, make full proof of thy ministry" (2 Timothy 4:5). In describing the ministry gifts of Christ to His body, the church, Paul listed evangelists along with apostles, prophets, pastors and teachers (see Ephesians 4:11). Luke records that Paul and his party visited Caesarea, where they abode with Philip the evangelist (see Acts 21:8).

While these three are the only specific New Testament references to the word *evangelist*, the root word from which it comes is mentioned repeatedly throughout the New Testament. The word *euaggelizo* occurs 53 times in the New Testament and the word *euaggelion* occurs 74 times. Translated as "preach the gospel" or "bring good tidings," these words always concern themselves with the good news of Christ's redeeming grace. Therefore, the word *evangelist* indicates one who is a preacher of the gospel of salvation. It is the evangelist's primary task to bring men and women to a saving knowledge of Jesus Christ.

The work of an evangelist is not a second-rate ministry. The evangelist is God's gift to the church. Evangelistic preaching is one of the gifted ministries necessary to produce a well-rounded church.

Although Philip is the only individual in the New Testament specifically referred to as an evangelist, many others were skilled in evangelistic preaching, and their works attest to this fact. Paul the apostle is often thought of as the calculating disciplinarian, the church leader, the missionary or the writer; but Paul was, in all probability, the greatest evangelistic preacher of all time.

Paul sought to preach to those who had never heard the good news, lest he should build on another man's foundation (see Romans 15:20). He planned his itinerary and his campaigns with the strategy of a general, preaching the gospel and planting churches in the major cities of his day.

Paul was such an evangelistic preacher that wherever he went he won people to Christ. Chain Paul to a prison guard and he wins the guard to Christ. Place him in Caesar's household and he writes, "The saints salute you, chiefly they that are of Caesar's household" (Philippians 4:22).

Put him in the presence of King Agrippa and the king cries out, "Almost thou persuadest me to be a Christian" (Acts 26:28).

Jail him at Philippi and at midnight he and Silas start a revival that sees the jailer converted and his entire household baptized (see 16:25-34).

Let Paul preach in the synagogue and chief rulers Crispus and Sosthenes leave their Jewish faith and turn to the church (see 18:8, 17).

Question Paul's apostleship, and he points to his converts and says, "Are not . . . [these] my work in the Lord? . . . the seal of mine apostleship" (1 Corinthians 9:1, 2). Or else he says, "Though ye have ten thousand instructors in Christ, yet have ye not many fathers: for in Christ Jesus I have begotten you through the gospel" (4:15).

Yes, Paul preached evangelistically!

What, then, are some chief characteristics of evangelistic preachers?

First, evangelistic preachers preach with a consuming zeal for the gospel and with compassion for the lost who need to hear the message. Like Paul, the effective evangelistic preacher must have passion in his soul. He must burn hot with fervor and enthusiasm, not content to move sluggishly about his task, as one strolling in the park on a Sunday afternoon, but as one rushing toward a great rendezvous with destiny. Like Jeremiah, with fire shut up in his bones, the evangelistic preacher must preach! Men must hear! They must be saved!

Second, the evangelistic preacher is conscious of a divine call that bids him specifically to win the lost. Some men teach, some lecture, some shepherd and care for the saints; but the evangelistic preacher has a calling special among men. He must go into the highways and byways of life. He must tell those who have never heard. He knows this to be his specific calling. Without such a consciousness, zeal will evaporate and the evangelistic preacher will turn elsewhere. Such passionate labor is extremely demanding.

Third, the evangelistic preacher is characterized by sensitivity to the Holy Spirit. He will rather close his sermon with a punch than preach on to make a point. The evangelistic preacher sees souls as his single objective and is willing to follow the Spirit down any road and into any corner for the purpose of winning another to the Lord. He may not always please the saints, he may not always conform to the normal way of doing things, he may not follow some set pattern of action in the worship service; but the evangelistic preacher will, if directed of God's Spirit, draw men to the Cross of Christ. That is his calling.

Fourth, the evangelistic preacher is characterized by deep convictions. He does not take the gospel lightly, nor is he willing to compromise with truths that deal with the eternal destiny of men. These convictions may be expressed forthrightly. They will usually be set forth in simple, straightforward language that is easily understood. Such is altogether proper and should be expected, for the theme of evangelistic preaching centers basically and primarily in John 3:16: "God so loved the world, that he gave his only begotten Son, that whosoever believeth in him should not perish, but have everlasting life."

Evangelistic preaching is positive about this message. The evangelistic preacher is not prejudiced, but he knows what he believes, he stands for it, and he is willing, if necessary, to die for it. He will say as Paul, "If any man preach any other gospel unto you than that ye have received, let him be accursed" (Galatians 1:9).

Preaching cannot convince others unless the man speaking is himself sold on the message.

Evangelistic Work Demands Character

What better place to start in evaluating the work of an evangelist than with the life and ministry of Philip? In the life of this deacon-turned-evangelist, one sees the strengths and traits of a noble man reflected.

Any minister whose life can approximate the character and the attributes of Philip should be productive in his evangelistic preaching.

Evangelistic Preaching Is Done by Men of Honest Report

Philip was a deacon-turned-evangelist, but he maintained his good reputation. It is tragic that the phrase "evangelistically speaking" has come to symbolize exaggeration and careless handling of truth. The opposite should be the case. God's men must always speak the truth and live what they preach.

Evangelistic Preachers Are Men Who Preach Christ

No better compliment can be paid any evangelist than for some to note, "He preaches Jesus."

Paul wrote to the Corinthians:

> For the Jews require a sign, and the Greeks seek after wisdom: But we preach Christ crucified, unto the Jews a stumbling block, and unto the Greeks foolishness; But unto them which are called, both Jews and Greeks, Christ the power of God, and the wisdom of God. Because the foolishness of God is wiser than men; and the weakness of God is stronger than men (1 Corinthians 1:22-25).

Again Paul wrote: "For I delivered unto you first of all that which I also received, how that Christ died for our sins according to the scriptures; And that he was buried, and that he rose again the third day according to the scriptures" (15:3, 4).

In Paul's second Corinthian epistle, we find the same theme:

> For we preach not ourselves, but Christ Jesus the Lord; and ourselves your servants for Jesus' sake. For God, who commanded the light to shine out of darkness, hath shined in our hearts, to give the light of the knowledge of the glory of God in the face of Jesus Christ. But we have this treasure in earthen vessels, that the excellency of the power may be of God, and not of us (4:5-7).

To crowds both large and small, in places heavily populated like Samaria (see Acts 8:5), or in the desert where he talked with one Ethiopian eunuch (see v. 35), Philip centered his words around the person of Jesus Christ. What the evangelistic preacher has to say, especially, must be centered in the Word of God. Only the Word creates faith. It is not miracles, signs, or wonders in themselves, but the Word that draws men to Christ. "Faith cometh by hearing, and hearing by the word of God" (Romans 10:17).

Someone has said that the evangelistic preaching of our day needs to be redeemed. It needs to be redeemed from the mouthing of platitudes, from pious insincerity, false tears, pulpit tones, and weak, pitiful attempts at dramatic effects. It needs to be redeemed from trickery in handling people and from the prostitution of so holy a thing as the gospel to unworthy ends. It needs to be redeemed from commercialization and men who make merchandise of people. It needs to be redeemed from cheap sensationalism and restored to the Biblical foundations of truth.

Evangelistic Preaching Will Often be Attested by Miracles

Just as with Peter, Paul, John and other New Testament evangelists, miracles followed in the wake of Philip's preaching. Supernatural manifestations, or miracles, do not supplant the Word, but they do complement it. Miracles confirm the Word. If people are to come to Christ, miracles must accompany the ministry of Pentecostal evangelists. Such is the Scriptural pattern (see Mark 16:20; Acts 9:35), and such should be expected rather than thought of as out of the ordinary.

Evangelistic Work Demands Joyful Preaching

Revival will lift people up, centering their eyes on heavenly things. The true gospel makes people sing and rejoice. Like sunlight breaking through clouds after a long, dreary winter day, evangelistic preaching warms the human heart. When Philip preached in Samaria, God's Word tells us, "There was great joy in that city" (8:8).

When Paul and Barnabas were persecuted and expelled from Antioch in Pisidia, the Scriptures depict the attitude of true evangelists with these words: "They shook off the dust of their feet against them, and came unto Iconium. And the disciples were filled with joy, and with the Holy Ghost" (13:51, 52).

Evangelistic Work Is Church Centered

Philip may have journeyed to Samaria alone, but he was not a loner. He remained conscious of his relationship with fellow believers in Jerusalem. At the same time, those men in Jerusalem were aware of Philip and of his mission to Samaria. When the Jerusalem elders heard of Philip's results, they sent Peter and John to help. Thus strengthened, the revival continued; and with it came an outpouring of the Holy Spirit similar to what happened on the Day of Pentecost. Any evangelism that does not begin with the church and, ultimately, return to the church will not be of a lasting nature.

Evangelistic Work Is Directed of the Spirit

"Then the Spirit said unto Philip, Go near, and join thyself to this chariot" (Acts 8:29). Those words are simple and clear. Philip heard the Spirit speaking and Philip obeyed. No evangelist can expect to win souls for Christ until, and unless, he preaches with the unction of God's Spirit. So long as men choose the time and the place, so long as men choose the occasion and the circumstances, then men will accomplish only what the wisdom of men is capable of doing. However, when the Spirit directs the preaching, what is accomplished will be miraculous and of eternal significance. God works with the speaker and the listener at the same time. God prepares the message and the recipient at the same moment. Evangelistic preachers obey God's Spirit.

Evangelistic Work Centers in Soulwinning

Philip did not view himself as a major campaign speaker only. He was not partial to great crowds or to big cities. He was willing to follow the Spirit into the desert, where he gave himself totally to the preaching of Christ to one man. It is unfortunate that many evangelists today become burdened for the lost only when they are in church or in the pulpit. They think their converts must be found in church alone, and they give little if any attention to witnessing outside the four walls of a traditional building. Personal soulwinning is not above or beyond the dignity of any evangelist: it is a ministry every preacher should seek to fulfill.

Evangelistic Preaching Includes Doctrine

Philip was not willing to leave his task unfinished. He was not one to forsake important spiritual considerations. Once the eunuch had accepted Christ, Philip stopped the chariot and baptized him. Evangelistic work today must also give attention to a follow-up ministry. Converts must be instructed in the Christian life. They must be baptized. They must be charged and directed into the fellowship of a local congregation rather than left alone as easy prey for the devil.

Does not the picture shape up? Can one not see in these Scriptural glimpses into Philip's preaching ministry what the pattern of evangelistic preaching should be?

This brings us to the most important element in evangelistic preaching—one's ability to bring hearers to commitment, to persuade them in reaching a verdict.

Evangelistic Preaching Centers in the Altar Call

Evangelistic preaching must be pointed. The preacher who blows a forgotten tune or who gives an uncertain sound on the gospel trumpet should not be surprised when men fail to respond. Perhaps it is true, as some say, that a few men are more gifted in the giving of the altar call than others; but this must not deter every minister from doing his best and from giving full attention to how and when he invites sinners to an altar of repentance. None should take lightly his altar-invitation responsibility.

There is strong and impressive Biblical premise for the invitation, or the altar call. Following Peter's sermon on the Day of Pentecost, the crowd was so stirred they said to Peter and the brethren, "What shall we do?" (Acts 2:37). Peter replied, "Repent, and be baptized every one of you in the name of Jesus Christ for the remission of sins" (v. 38).

Some men preach until listeners are convicted and then fail to tell sinners what to do.

Jesus began His ministry with a call to repentance: "The time is fulfilled, and the kingdom of God is at hand: repent ye, and believe the gospel" (Mark 1:15). Jesus always spoke for decision. He forced men to choose. "Follow me," Jesus said. "Come after me . . . Believe in me . . . Come unto me."

It is theologically correct to call men to repentance. Man's acceptance before God is predicated upon man's response to the gospel. It is man who must choose: "Come unto me, all ye that labour and are heavy laden, and I will give you rest" (Matthew 11:28).

John sets forth the theological dilemma most clearly when he quotes the Lord's words: "All that the Father giveth me shall come to me; and him that cometh to me I will in no wise cast out" (John 6:37).

God convicts men of their sin, God's Holy Spirit persuades men to accept Christ, and the Word cuts deeply into men's consciousness; but it yet remains for each individual to bow his will to Christ. Thus, evangelistic preaching must give attention to persuasion, a holy and awesome task.

Perhaps here, more than anywhere else, the attitude of the evangelist is important. Evangelistic preachers are men of compassion. They speak with love and concern. Although their message is one of judgment as well as grace, they yearn for the sinner to turn to God. This yearning is expressed in voice and in attitude, heightened by the power of the Spirit.

Paul wrote to the Romans: "Brethren, my heart's desire and prayer to God for Israel is, that they might be saved" (Romans 10:1).

Paul's compassion was set forth even more explicitly when he wrote to the Thessalonians:

> Nor of men sought we glory, neither of you, nor yet of others. . . . But we were gentle among you, even as a nurse cherisheth her children: So being affectionately desirous of you, we were willing to have imparted unto you, not the gospel of God only, but also our own souls, because ye were dear unto us (1 Thessalonians 2:6-8).

"The love of Christ constraineth us," Paul wrote in 2 Corinthians 5:14.

Such is the compassion and the spirit of evangelistic preaching.

Here are a few simple suggestions for making altar calls effective. Some of these are matters that good evangelists do naturally or by the leading of God's Holy Spirit; but these considerations sometimes go unnoticed.

First, one should see that the altar invitation is properly timed. Every sermon will have its climactic moment, that precise point when all arguments and all words peak. In a particular service, this moment may or may not be when and where the preacher anticipates. The Holy Spirit may direct it along different lines. Nevertheless, the climax is when the invitation should be made. Some men lose impact by continuing to preach or by stopping too soon. Timing is vital for response.

Timing the altar call has often been compared to the skill of fishing; one must know precisely when to sink the hook, or the fish will be lost. Evangelists are fishers of men.

Second, one should make the altar invitation definite. Leave no doubt in the listener's mind as to what he must do. It is impossible for men and women to respond if they are not sure what is being asked. Some ministers make their appeal too general. The good evangelist lays his challenge before the people in living color. He makes it plain. He is specific with his instruction.

Third, one should be prepared for the transition from sermon to altar invitation. See that transition takes place smoothly. Have the music selected and the musicians prepared. Avoid lost motion or any sideline activity that might distract the sinner's attention.

Fourth, one should decide when the invitation will conclude. The evangelist alone must make this decision. Invitations vary in length. There are times when they should be extended; other times they should be closed with a punch, emphasizing the urgency of the hour. Whichever, the evangelist must make the decision. When he has done so, he should urge the people to respond. One may assist this decision process either with a change of song or by directing a change of position on the part of the audience.

Finally, one should be prepared to instruct those who respond to the invitation. It may be that the evangelist handles this personally, or he may train altar workers to assist him; but those who come forward ought to have someone to give them instructions, assisting them in their acceptance of the Lord. Some people do not know how to pray. They are very self-conscious in their attempts. Others need to better understand the steps of salvation. While he may have explained such steps in the closing moments of his sermon, the evangelistic preacher will also follow through, in the altar, not hesitating to be down among seekers, explaining and leading them through to salvation.

Then there must be follow-up. The new convert needs further instruction and prayer. He needs to be established in the faith and to have definite contact with the pastor, the church and other members of the congregation.

Whether the preacher is a full-time evangelist or a pastor who preaches evangelistically on Sunday nights, these suggestions will help bear fruit. All ministers must on occasion become evangelistic preachers. All must give themselves to the winning of the lost. At this point the preacher faces his greatest challenge and discharges his greatest responsibility. By all means, he must win some.

Evangelistic Preachers Help Train Others

There is another aspect of evangelism—a concrete and precise New Testament aspect of evangelism—which should be emphasized in these closing paragraphs. It is doubtful that many readers disagree with the concept that lay persons also are charged with some responsibility for the winning of the lost. The purpose here will not be to set forth arguments for lay evangelism, but rather to remind readers of the rationale for such a ministry and of how woefully lacking it has become in some churches.

Although some change has been apparent during the past few years, ministers largely do not assume their responsibility for recruiting, training and sending forth laymen into the harvest. One often hears the complaint that sinners do not come to church as they once did. Why not? One reason is that Christian believers are not out witnessing, telling neighbors and fellow workers about God's goodness.

In the early days of modern Pentecost, contrary to some thinking, sinners did not come to church because they had nothing better to do. They came because they saw what was taking place in the lives of their neighbors. They came because mothers, dads, brothers and sisters suddenly started living differently. They came because some Christian stopped them on the street and told of miraculous things happening at the tent revival. By and large, it was not the great preaching that brought those revivals, it was the witnessing of converts and Spirit-filled saints during work hours and between services. Everywhere they went, following the New Testament pattern, early Pentecostals told of the goodness and greatness of Christ in their lives. Their witness stirred hearts.

Revivals will come again to the church when believers return to this New Testament pattern. Churches will fill again when saints follow the program the disciples set forth in the Book of Acts. Their pattern has very little to do with four walls, high-steepled churches, and services scheduled for Sunday morning, Sunday evening and Wednesday night. The New Testament pattern has much to do with recruitment, training and the sending forth of witnesses into the world.

One fact stands out in stark contrast to events in the Book of Acts: many have taken too lightly the pastor's responsibility, and the evangelistic preacher's responsibility, to teach and to train laymen to witness. Ministers have permitted their members to join that great silent majority of believers who attend church, who live honestly, who are good neighbors and who never disturb anyone. In doing this, churches have strayed from the New Testament pattern, forgetting that it is through the sharing of faith that the vibrancy of faith rekindles itself.

One pastor shared the burden of his heart in noting that, if he had his last pastorate to do over—a pastorate which, in many ways, was a successful one the one thing he would do is train new converts in the art of lay evangelism. He noted that most of his converts were won to Christ outside the church rather than through regular services. He acknowledged that, if he had only a dozen committed men and women, he could have accomplished much more for the kingdom of God.

Summary

It would seem that the word *minister*, as used in the Bible, speaks of the pulpit and the pew. In a very real sense, all believers are ministers. All must realize that the Great Commission strikes pulpit and pew at the same angle. All are charged with being Christ's witnesses.

Men should give more attention to preaching for souls. Ministers are first of all evangelistic preachers, and they must therefore do the work of evangelism. This means following the example of Philip, Paul and other New Testament evangelists, especially in firmness and conviction of altar invitations. However, it also means training lay persons to go forth with the good news of Christ for a dying world.

Pentecostal Preaching Is Prophetic

Introduction

In a measure, the Golden Age of the prophets had passed away and the prophetic gift had become comparatively rare when Joel came on the scene 24 generations before Pentecost.

The Hebrew people lived in the glory of past prophets. They, no doubt, wondered if an era of power such as that demonstrated through Elijah and Elisha would ever return to Israel. Although the days were dark, the man of God—as prophets were called in that era—received a message of hope for his people:

> Be glad then, ye children of Zion, and rejoice in the Lord your God: for he hath given you the former rain moderately, and he will cause to come down for you the rain, the former rain, and the latter rain in the first month. And the floors shall be full of wheat, and the vats shall overflow

> with wine and oil. And I will restore to you the
> years that the locust hath eaten, the canker-
> worm, and the caterpillar, and the palmerworm,
> my great army which I sent among you.
>
> And ye shall eat in plenty, and be satisfied, and
> praise the name of the Lord your God, that hath
> dealt wondrously with you: and my people shall
> never be ashamed. And ye shall know that I am
> in the midst of Israel, and that I am the Lord
> your God, and none else: and my people shall
> never be ashamed. And it shall come to pass
> afterward, that I will pour out my spirit upon all
> flesh; and your sons and your daughters shall
> prophesy, your old men shall dream dreams,
> your young men shall see visions: And also
> upon the servants and upon the handmaids in
> those days will I pour out my spirit (Joel 2:23-29).

Above and beyond the temporal blessings mentioned, there was to be an outpouring of the Spirit that
would be accompanied by the prophetic gift in a most
unusual manner. Sons and daughters of the family, as
well as servants of the household, were to become par-
takers of the Spirit that made Elijah and Elisha stand
head and shoulders above others of their day.

Joel prophesied of an age of blessing when the
prophetic unction was to be shared by many. The essential facts of his prediction were these: first, a great age of
salvation was to be opened; second, this coming era
would be distinguished by the gift of the Holy Ghost;
third, the presence of the Holy Spirit was to be marked
by an extraordinary manifestation of prophetic power.

Pentecostal Preaching Is Prophetic Preaching

Prophecy was thus promised to be a distinctive gift of Pentecost. No one, can doubt that the 120 at Pentecost were endowed with divine energy and speech such as was not known before. According to the message of the apostle Peter, Joel's prophecy was specifically fulfilled:

> And it shall come to pass in the last days, saith God, I will pour out of my Spirit upon all flesh: and your sons and your daughters shall prophesy, and your young men shall see visions, and your old men shall dream dreams: And on my servants and on my handmaidens I will pour out in those days of my Spirit; and they shall prophesy (Acts 2:17, 18).

Since the Spirit assigned such prominence to this prophetic gift, it is certainly worthy of our consideration today.

Like some other Scriptural terms, the word *prophesy* has, by popular usage, acquired a restricted meaning. When the King James Version of the Bible was published, the words *prophesy* and *preach* were so similar in meaning that they could be used interchangeably. Modern usage of the word *prophesy* is understood to mean almost exclusively the predicting of future events. As a result, the full force of the Scriptural term is not generally understood or appreciated.

The predictive element is certainly not absent from New Testament prophecy, but a more accurate definition is "forthtelling." In the Scriptural sense, the New Testament prophet is one empowered by authority of the Holy Ghost to declare the mind of God. He therefore proclaims truth put in his heart by the Holy Ghost. This brings us to the more correct definition of prophesy, which makes the minister one who speaks for another: The prophet speaks for God. Not only does he receive authority to speak through the Spirit, but his message comes through the Holy Spirit as well. He is moved by the Spirit to speak. His heart is strangely warmed by the Spirit. His mind is illuminated by the Spirit to deliver the message which God sends through him. The Holy Ghost quickens his mental powers, guides his thoughts, and moves him to deal in certain topics of need. This is preaching prophetically. This is Pentecostal preaching at its best.

Rarely does the divine message come as though dictated from God. The Holy Spirit moves upon the Pentecostal preacher and he speaks in his own words those things revealed to him, or impressed upon his mind, by the Spirit. Sometimes the message comes by revelation. At other times the Spirit brings to the preacher's remembrance certain things he has studied and learned—things which are appropriate for the moment.

For this reason, prophetic preaching does not preclude study and preparation. The Spirit, except through revelation, cannot bring to one's mind that which the mind has not learned. "But the Comforter, which is the Holy Ghost, whom the Father will send in my name," Jesus said, "he shall teach you all things, and bring all things to your remembrance, whatsoever I have said unto you" (John 14:26).

The prophet retains command of his vocal and mental powers and acts as a responsible agent both in what he says and does not say. "The spirits of the prophets are subject to the prophets" (1 Corinthians 14:32). This being true, Pentecostal preaching requires a yielded vessel, one sensitive to the Spirit and to the needs of people. Total reliance upon the Spirit is necessary to reach this plateau of preaching. While the preacher has notes, outlines, or even a manuscript, he must keep himself open for God's Spirit to direct him at the moment.

Sometimes the Spirit will lead the Pentecostal preacher in another direction just to meet a specific need of someone in the congregation. At this point, it is necessary for the preacher to abandon notes and to speak extemporaneously, directed by the Spirit. The Pentecostal preacher must be willing for God to use him as a mouthpiece. The pride of a preacher's heart or the fear of failure may prevent him from total dependence on the Spirit, but some of the best sermons are born while a man is preaching under the unction of the Spirit.

The Spirit often leads the anointed minister to deal with a point that later develops into a full sermon.

There is no greater thrill for a preacher than to know God is illuminating his mind and that, through inspiration, he is speaking from God to men. At such a moment, thoughts rush on him: he can hardly speak before other thoughts present themselves for consideration. Scriptures previously read and studied are brought to memory and unfold in beautiful splendor and symmetry. Once a minister experiences this type of preaching, he is never quite satisfied with less. This is why prayer and fasting are so essential to Pentecostal preaching. It is through prayer and fasting that the minister remains sensitive to the Spirit, thus maintaining his fresh anointing.

After one has preached for a number of years, there is danger of relying on past experiences and on human knowledge that has been accumulated. Preaching may become perfunctory and lose its fresh touch. Each man must constantly evaluate his preaching in order to remain effective and productive.

The prophet of God is commissioned from on high to reprove, rebuke, exhort; to proclaim God's promises to the wicked, as well as the righteous; to guide the weak and wandering; to comfort the sorrowing and, in short, to speak in God's stead to the people. When God speaks through the minister, the message will sometimes evoke disfavor. Unless the preacher is a man of courage, he will be unable to deliver God's message with necessary effectiveness. Courage is a special gift of anointing—a spiritual gift that prepares a man for a difficult task. There is need to preach with boldness. The apostles prayed, "Grant unto thy servants, that with all boldness they may speak thy word" (Acts 4:29).

God's response to that prayer was unforgettable: "The place was shaken where they were assembled together; and they were all filled with the Holy Ghost, and they spake the word of God with boldness. . . . With great power gave the apostles witness of the resurrection of the Lord Jesus" (vv. 31, 33).

During the Lord's trial and crucifixion, Peter was not a man of much courage either spiritually or morally. After his Upper Room experience, Peter stood up on the morning of Pentecost and spoke like a man incapable of fear. The unction of the Spirit can make timid men brave, furnishing them with the necessary boldness of a prophet. There are times when the Pentecostal preacher must have courage to speak as Nathan the prophet spoke, "Thou art the man" (2 Samuel 12:7). Sometimes he must speak as did Peter to Ananias and Sapphira: "Thou hast not lied unto men, but unto God" (Acts 5.4).

Pentecostal preaching is heart-searching and piercing because it is the preaching of the Word:

> For the word of God is quick, and powerful, and sharper than any two-edged sword, piercing even to the dividing asunder of soul and spirit, and of the joints and marrow, and is a discerner of the thoughts and intents of the heart (Hebrews 4:12).

Many things that people suppose to be hidden are brought to light through prophetic preaching. This phase of the prophetic gift is illustrated in Paul's first letter to the Christians at Corinth:

> But if all prophesy, and there come in one that believeth not, or one unlearned, he is convinced of all, he is judged of all: And thus are the secrets of his heart made manifest; and so falling down on his face he will worship God, and report that God is in you of a truth (1 Corinthians 14:24, 25).

Anointed preaching is so penetrating that Pentecostal ministers are sometimes accused of preaching at people or indulging in personalities. Friends are accused of having told the preacher about them. This is simply the Spirit speaking to the needs of individuals and convicting them of sins.

The Spirit often reveals the needs of a congregation to the preacher. While this is a rewarding and humbling experience, it may also be frightening because of the responsibility it places on the minister's shoulders.

Possibly the most conspicuous weakness in today's preaching is the absence of this element of prophecy. Comparatively few preachers speak with the authority of an anointed prophet. Instead of setting the pace for public opinion, they all too often tend to follow it.

The First Pentecostal Sermon Is an Example of Prophetic Preaching

God chose the apostle Peter to deliver the first Pentecostal sermon. In Peter's recorded text one finds sparkling gems of divine wisdom too beautiful and perfect to be ascribed solely to the man speaking. Peter spoke with the unction of the Holy Spirit. He spoke in the tradition and manner of great Old Testament prophets. He spoke at the behest and under the direction of the Holy Spirit. Thus, his sermon must be recognized as prophetic preaching.

Before examining Peter's sermon, one does well to note some peculiarities of the occasion—some distinctives that differ from the mood and the tone of the historical narrative up to Pentecost. These facts stand out.

First, it was the gift of the Spirit, the outpouring of the Holy Ghost, that set the stage for that first Pentecostal sermon. Many visitors had come to Jerusalem, but it was divine providence and the Pentecostal phenomenon that gathered the crowd to whom Peter preached.

Second—and to most Bible scholars this seems equally clear—Peter was empowered and emboldened to speak as a direct result of the Holy Spirit having come upon him. For Peter, things had changed dramatically during the past 50 days. He had met the risen Christ, he had been forgiven and restored, he had witnessed the

Ascension, and he had been to the Upper Room. Now, unctionized and empowered by the Holy Spirit, he becomes God's mouthpiece.

Third, Peter centered his preaching and based his arguments upon the Word. He referred to scriptures about which most people present had some knowledge. In Peter's exegesis of Psalm 16:8-11, one sees not the temperamental and fickle apostle of old but the transformed and anointed Pentecostal preacher with wisdom and words beyond himself.

Fourth, Peter's sermon magnified and centered in Jesus Christ. Humanly speaking, this was not the moment for a public speaker to be referring to One who had so recently been put to an ignominious death; but Peter got right to the point. He laid the matter of Jesus Christ, and of his divine appointment and approval, at the listeners' feet. Peter placed on those present the guilt for that death, and he called them to repentance in Christ's own name.

Finally, it must be noted that the first Pentecostal sermon produced miraculous and unprecedented results. Pentecostal preaching today—prophetic preaching to this generation—when following the same pattern, when emphasizing the same points, when directed of the same Spirit, will produce similar results.

Let us now look closer at Peter's sermon. It is obvious that not every sermon will be placed within so spectacular a setting as this one. One should recognize, however, that the God who created the circumstances of that first sermon is the same God who providentially works in the affairs of men today. In other words, God does not wait for the preacher to get there and for a man to speak before He begins preparing hearts and setting the stage for His message. Thus, Pentecostal preachers, those who preach prophetically, may always step into the pulpit with a consciousness of divine appointment. God prepares the occasion in advance.

Introduction and Opening Remarks

Peter began his sermon with a straightforward and practical explanation of what was taking place. Those who had gathered were curious and puzzled. They knew something of an unusual nature was happening, and some theorized that the believers were drunk. Peter quickly dispelled the thoughts about drunkenness and noted, "This is that which was spoken by the prophet Joel" (Acts 2:16).

This example argues well for relevancy. Prophetic preaching gets to the point at hand. It addresses itself to the immediate question.

"This is that promised blessing of which Joel spoke," Peter said. "God is pouring out His Spirit upon all flesh. Your sons and your daughters shall prophesy. Your young men shall see visions. Your old men shall dream dreams. Your servants and your handmaidens will also receive the Spirit and they too shall prophesy" (Joel 2:28, 29; paraphrased).

With that skillful call to attention, Peter noted that other signs were forthcoming. He added that all who called upon the name of the Lord would be saved.

The Holy Spirit Has Come to Testify of Jesus Christ

Jesus of Nazareth was the topic of Peter's sermon, and Jesus was a subject with which many of the people were familiar already. In reference to Jesus, Peter spoke of four truths: His approval by God, His open life, His miraculous works and His undeniable report.

"Ye yourselves know this," Peter said.

Peter's theology was broad enough for him to note that Jesus of Nazareth died "by the determinate counsel and foreknowledge of God." His theology was at the same time applicable enough for him to tell his hearers, "Ye have taken, and by wicked hands have crucified and slain [Him]" (Acts 2:23).

This same Jesus God has raised up, God has loosed from death; for it was not possible that He, the Son of God, should be held captive to death.

Reference to a Familiar Passage of Old Testament Scripture

Most of the listeners that day would have been familiar with Psalm 16:8-11. All were aware of King David. Thus Peter's reference to his nation's most glorious king was a reference immediately understood. "It was David himself who told of the Messiah's kingship after resurrection," Peter said. Then he pointed out clearly how the psalmist could not have been writing of himself, for David was dead and those present knew where his tomb was located. David had prophesied of the Messiah. Jesus Christ of Nazareth was the fruit of God's promise to David (see Acts 2:30).

One may judge Peter's sermon from any angle, and it shapes up as a marvelous example of prophetic preaching. Even from the human point of view, one notices the order by which Peter, the speaker, took the people from that which was known already toward that which he wished to prove; and how he, through the Spirit, used their own arguments to make his case.

The Authenticity of Christ's Resurrection

Not only did the prophets tell of Jesus in advance, Peter said, and not only did David prophesy of His resurrection, but Peter and the other disciples were witnesses of this miracle. "We have seen the risen, resurrected, living Lord in person. Jesus of Nazareth has returned to the Father, He has sat down at the Father's right hand, and He has shed forth this [the Holy Spirit] which ye see and hear" (Acts 2:33; paraphrased).

In his speaking, Peter turned full circle. He started with reference to the outpouring of the Spirit and concluded by returning to the same relevant subject.

"Therefore," Peter said, "let all the house of Israel know assuredly, that God hath made that same Jesus, whom ye have crucified, both Lord and Christ" (v. 36).

It was not a long sermon. It was not a rambling sermon. It was not a sermon filled with unnecessary frills. It was a sermon driven home by the power and the cutting force of God's Holy Spirit. Here one sees the limits of man's ability and, to be quite honest, the limits of man's responsibility. Peter could do no more Peter had spoken the message of God. Peter had delivered his soul in accordance with the Holy Spirit. That is when the Spirit did His work, when the Holy Spirit drove the message into the hearts of those listening. The Bible says, "When they heard this, they were pricked in their heart" (v. 37).

They saw themselves as guilty and lost. They wanted Peter to tell them what to do.

The Sermon's Conclusion

Peter was prepared. His conclusion, too, was masterful, consisting of three imperatives. First, "Repent of your sins." Second, "Believe on Christ for the remission of your sins, and express your faith and commitment by baptism in His name." Third, "Receive the gift of the Holy Spirit for yourselves."

Pentecostal preaching, prophetic preaching, must never convince people of what is wrong without telling them what to do. The preacher who is anointed of the Holy Spirit will be a preacher who drives this point home hard and fast.

Peter did so with great effectiveness: "The same day there were added unto them about three thousand souls" (v. 41).

Depends Upon the Holy Spirit

Prophetic preaching today, just as in Biblical times, depends totally on the power of the Holy Spirit.

We see the divine pattern repeated when Philip went to Samaria for a revival (see Acts 8:5-8), and when Peter visited in the home of Cornelius (see 10:34-48). In these examples, the results of preaching are clearly attributable to the Holy Spirit.

The preacher who would preach prophetically must be a man sensitive to the Holy Spirit. He must move with the Spirit, not too fast and not too slowly. He must be constantly tuned in, always willing to yield, to change, to do things differently at the Spirit's bidding. Being thus, his words take on new and unprecedented effectiveness. They cut when seeming to be dull. They pierce when not obviously pointed. They convict when not outwardly dramatic. Because they are of the Holy Spirit, they pierce with the Spirit's power.

Prophetic preaching produces results. Such preaching trims and prunes in a manner not always obvious. The Pentecostal preacher is especially blessed by being an instrument in this type ministry. By and large, he is the beneficiary of progress and results more glorious and more rewarding than he has right to expect. Whether he sees these results or not, he can rest assured that God is using the Word, that God is taking the message and applying it to hearts for divine purpose. This alone makes preaching a glorious experience.

Many men have tried to describe Pentecostal preaching. Many have attempted to put into words the emotions experienced by a man under heavy unction and anointing of the Holy Spirit. It is not an easy experience to tell about. This author has wrestled with the explanation for years and has always found words poor and inadequate vehicles for capturing the high emotional impact of such a moment in the pulpit.

Ian MacPherson puts it this way: "It is the surge of divine power through a personality selfless enough to permit its fullest, unrestricted flow, a surge of power so terrific in its impact upon the congregation that, before it, every lofty imagination is brought low and every thought taken captive to the obedience of Christ."

Most readers of these pages will agree that preaching depends on the Holy Spirit for its power and effectiveness. It is another thing altogether to address ourselves to the question of how the human instrument yields to the Spirit, and how the preacher positions himself to work with the Spirit, thus making his preaching more exemplary and powerful. If preaching is to ring with prophetic impact, there is a role for the instrument to play. There is a choice to be made, a commitment to keep.

The Yielded Vessel

The question is not whether the power of the Holy Spirit is present or adequate, but whether we are in tune with the Spirit and used of Him. Some men are used more dramatically than others. This may, at times, mean these men are especially chosen or positioned, as with Peter on the Day of Pentecost; or it may mean they have been praying and are in the proper frame of mind, the proper attitude to hear the Spirit's message.

One must be very careful on this point. It is not right to imply that the more dramatic preaching, or the more open and ostentatious styles, are necessarily the most anointed and most effective sermons. Such may not be true at all. What needs to be said, and repeated, is that the work of God's Spirit in a human vessel is determined to a great extent by the vessel's yieldedness, and by the willingness of the human instrument to follow the Spirit.

What steps are open to the minister today? What are some of the things God's men should consider if they want to be more effective preachers, and desire to preach prophetically more often and with more results?

It is not carnal to desire such. The man of God should be genuinely concerned about the kingdom of God. This concern should move him to his best, motivating him to actions which produce fruitful ministry.

Here are some suggestions for the Spirit-filled, prophetic preacher.

1. *One should cultivate his personal relationship with Christ.* A man cannot preach Christ unless a man knows Christ intimately. This relationship is altogether personal and must be cultivated on a daily and hourly basis. Christ is a living presence. He is with His people

always, in all situations, and under all circumstances; and those who preach and tell others must not neglect their own souls.

Although he had served the Lord long and faithfully, Paul expressed the deepest desire of his heart when he wrote to his beloved church in Philippi, "That I may know him, and the power of his resurrection, and the fellowship of his sufferings, being made conformable unto his death" (Philippians 3:10). Prophetic preachers, men who preach with power and effectiveness, are men who know Jesus Christ in a continuing, daily relationship. People will take knowledge of them that they have been with Jesus (see Acts 4:13.)

2. *One should practice intercessory prayer.* Intercessory prayer is one way to move obstacles. Intercessory prayer will change the mind and the heart of people; it will eradicate opposition and set the stage for a powerful infusion of God's Spirit, through the Word.

We have stated already that this generation needs more productive and precise preaching, but it also needs more intercessory prayer by warriors who wrestle with the powers of evil and then emerge from secret closets powerfully and dramatically charged with a message. Preaching under the anointing of the Holy Spirit is the sword thrust that convicts, but prayer sets the stage and prepares human hearts to hear that Word.

3. *One should seek God for a message, not just a sermon.* There is a vast difference. Sermons are structured and may take many forms. Messages are precise and to the point. Messages may be conveyed in different ways, but they cut and change lives. A sermon may be something memorized, something outlined, something vaguely and humanly satisfying; but a message burns,

it aches, it invokes to tears, it sends a man to the pulpit without pretense and without defense and bursts forth as a force that cannot be restrained.

When God gives a man a message for His people, it may be necessary to couch that message in many sermons. The message may be repeated, with different passages of Scripture and with different nuances, but it will be a message from the throne and the preacher will not desist until there is fruit. The minister must know in his heart what the message of the hour really is. Only then will he preach prophetically and with Pentecostal power.

4. *One should speak from his heart and soul.* If the message does not move the preacher, it will not move others. The Pentecostal preacher's heart must burn with love, with compassion, with the urgency of the hour. Only then will men and women turn to Christ. Not every speaker will be equally dynamic, not every preacher will be blessed with a loud and impressive voice or with a commanding physique; but every preacher of the gospel can and ought to be totally honest when he steps behind the sacred desk. He should speak from his heart and feel first what he hopes others to see and hear through his words.

5. *One should ask God to direct his performance in the pulpit.* This should not be a perfunctory request. It should be the sincere desire and prayer of every man going to the pulpit. By so seeking, a man prepares himself for accepting the answer and obeying the Spirit. A man thus goes into the pulpit with a consciousness of divine mission and with the belief that God will direct him. He takes one more step toward powerful, prophetic preaching.

A man should also evaluate his own preaching. He should look closely at how he performs, at how he goes about the preaching task. He should lay himself before the Lord and ask God to do an evaluation on him. When God gets through with His examination, one may find his grade less than satisfactory, and one may go at the next task with an altogether different attitude.

6. *One should always be sensitive to the Spirit.* God seldom thunders. He does not often knock a man down and force him to listen. Men must give an ear to God. Men must wait upon, and be patient with, the Spirit. To follow the whispering of God's Spirit is more glorious than to follow the loud voice of popular opinion. Even when the Spirit leads one against the current, or when the Spirit sends one into the dark wood or into the dangerous bog, it is still better to follow Him. The way of self is the sure road to failure and destruction.

7. *One should be bold in his obedience.* Once the Spirit speaks, the man of God should obey Him. Some men stall, others doubt, some step forward tentatively, as if they are not sure God knows His business. But the Pentecostal preacher, the Spirit-anointed preacher, goes forth with the boldness of a lion. Such a preacher would rather venture and lose than not venture at all.

Such a preacher will accomplish great and miraculous things for the Kingdom: "For God hath not given us the spirit of fear; but of power, and of love, and of a sound mind" (2 Timothy 1:7).

Boldness and Pentecost are partners. They go hand in hand. They mark the prophetic preacher.

8. *Finally, one should expect results when he preaches.* Some men convey in their attitude and with their expressions that they really do not expect results. That

man who preaches prophetically, under the anointing of the Spirit, is a man who expects men and women to be moved. He expects response and prepares for it.

Ironically, some men talk about dramatic results but prepare for little. They are like a man requesting a large offering but then passing around a small offering plate.

Summary

Preaching at its best is *prophetic*, meaning "forth-telling" rather than exclusively referring to the predicting of future events. Such preaching was demonstrated by Peter's sermon on the Day of Pentecost; and such preaching is possible today for the Spirit-filled, inspired, anointed Pentecostal preacher.

Preaching may occur under varying circumstances and in many guises and styles; but preaching is never perfect, never at its best, *until* and *unless* the messenger, through the Holy Spirit, becomes literally the mouthpiece of God. Such is what men become when they prayerfully dedicate themselves to the gospel and when they sincerely and honestly give themselves to the Scriptures.

9

The Uniqueness of Pentecostal Preaching

Introduction

Pentecostal preaching is so unique in its nature and so encompassing in its power that no word other than "supernatural" seems adequate to describe it.

Pentecostal preaching today has the same power and authority it evidenced on the Day of Pentecost nearly 2,000 years ago. Pentecostal preaching today will produce the same miraculous results it produced during the early days of the New Testament church. It is the same uniting of human instrument and divine power, the same blending of human commitment and phenomenal results as set forth in the Book of Acts. It is no more; it is no less.

Thus, the word *supernatural* is used herein to refer to signs, wonders, healings, and miracles such as happened during New Testament times.

Not only will Pentecostal preaching produce the same miraculous results as those recorded in the New

Testament, it will always produce them in keeping with the spirit and the tone of the New Testament. It is precisely for this reason that Pentecostals emphasize so strongly a belief in the "whole Bible, rightly divided."

Three points should be reiterated here:

1. True Pentecostal preaching always centers in the Word
2. Pentecostal preaching always exalts Jesus Christ
3. Pentecostal preaching is always directed and empowered by the Holy Spirit.

So long as these three basic guidelines are kept in perspective, one need have little fear of fanaticism or heresy. These guidelines will keep the man of God on track, sensitive to God's will, always promoting the church and the Kingdom rather than personal or earthly ambitions.

More important, these guidelines combine to make a man better than he is by nature. They give the Pentecostal preacher an advantage other men fail to realize or appreciate and, at the same time, they permit men to enjoy partnership with God in a special relationship.

Before noting specifically a few of the miracles that take place in the wake of Pentecostal preaching, let us remember that *signs, wonders, powers* and *works* were terms applied to the ministry of Jesus Christ. These were the evidences by which Jesus verified His claim to Messiahship. These were also the evidences found in the New Testament church as recorded in the Book of Acts. These evidences *should* and *will* follow true believers in the 21st century:

> [Jesus) said unto them, "Go ye into all the world, and preach the gospel to every creature. He that

believeth and is baptized shall be saved; but he
that believeth not shall be damned. And these
signs shall follow them that believe; In my name
shall they cast out devils; they shall speak with
new tongues; They shall take up serpents; and if
they drink any deadly thing, it shall not hurt
them; they shall lay hands on the sick, and they
shall recover." . . . And they went forth, and
preached every where, the Lord working with
them, and confirming the word with signs following (Mark 16:15-18, 20).

Pentecostal Preaching Convicts of Sin and Produces Revival

Pentecostal preaching is not predicated upon human
assumptions. Rather, it builds upon the Word, according to the leading of the Holy Spirit, and depends upon
the Spirit to convict and bring miraculous results.

Such has happened over and again in this author's
personal ministry. Even while the message was in
progress, men or women have been known to cry out,
to stand, and to run forward to an altar of prayer, conviction too heavy for them to wait. Many times these
individuals—so the author learned subsequently—
were people thought to be either in fellowship with God
or totally immune to the invitation. A pastor or some
friend would say afterwards, "I never would have sus-
pected he or she was struggling with such a burden."

These matters are not humanly known; they are discerned of the Holy Spirit. They illustrate the miracle
element in Pentecostal preaching. They remind us that
wherever and whenever there is Pentecostal preaching, revival is possible.

Pentecostal Preaching Moves Men and Women to be Baptized With the Holy Ghost

Throughout our world there is renewed interest in the person and work of the Holy Spirit. While some men propose to instruct seekers in receiving the baptism of the Holy Ghost, and others emphasize the human elements of submission and obedience, let it be noted that the New Testament gives preaching a prominent role in Pentecostal outpourings.

At the conclusion of his Pentecostal sermon, when Peter was asked what his hearers should do, he answered: "Repent, and be baptized every one of you in the name of Jesus Christ for the remission of sins, and ye shall receive the gift of the Holy Ghost. For the promise is unto you, and to your children, and to all that are afar off, even as many as the Lord our God shall call" (Acts 2: 38, 39).

At the home of Cornelius, what is often referred to as the Gentile Pentecost, took place. While Peter was in the middle of a Pentecostal sermon, "the Holy Ghost fell on all them which heard the word" (10:44).

While one would not wish to imply that it is only during preaching that men and women receive the Baptism—both Scripture and experience confirm that people receive the baptism of the Holy Spirit under varying circumstances—neither should one forget that such is a New Testament pattern. A powerful, anointed sermon centers the listener's heart and soul on things eternal; it points one heavenward; it stirs hope and faith; and, quite often, it inspires one to believe and accept the promised gift of the Holy Spirit.

Time and again this author has seen the Holy Ghost fall upon believers during the message, just as He fell upon believers while Peter spoke at the home of Cornelius. A case in point was during a message delivered at a camp meeting in Doraville, Georgia. Spontaneously the Spirit swept over the audience and some believers received the baptism of the Holy Ghost while they were in their seats; some stood with upraised hands and received the gift; while others received the Spirit en route to the altar. Forty souls received the baptism of the Holy Ghost in that service. The experience of Pentecost was repeated. The Holy Ghost fell on them as on believers at the beginning (see 11:15).

Another divine interruption was experienced as this author spoke at the Roberto Clemente Coliseum in San Juan, Puerto Rico. More than 200 people received the gift of the Holy Ghost in a single service! Pentecost indeed!

Pentecostal Preaching Produces Faith

Christian faith, saving faith, is of divine origin. Not only is this truth set forth explicitly in the Scriptures—"For by grace are ye saved through faith; and that not of yourselves: it is the gift of God" (Ephesians 2:8)—but it is likewise verified through human experience. In many of our lives, at one time we accepted the historical fact that Jesus Christ lived, died and was the Savior of the world; but, at the same time, we continued in our rebellion and were not Christians. Then came that moment of divine confrontation, that moment of conviction, that moment when faith rooted and when, somehow, we knew and believed personally that Jesus was Lord and Savior.

It was the Word that sparked our faith. We may not have been converted during the preaching of a sermon, or even in a church building, but it was the Word—what Paul referred to as "the power of God unto salvation" (Romans 1:16)—that planted the seed of faith; and it was the Holy Spirit who inseminated that seed and brought forth a new creation in Christ Jesus.

So it is with other manifestations of faith. The Word produces faith, and there are few moments when, or few places where, the Word is more piercingly sent forth than during an anointed, Pentecostal sermon.

During one of this author's messages in Pacific Palisades, California, the Spirit hovered over the audience. It was evident that God was present to do some miraculous things among us. As the people lifted their hands toward heaven, they were urged to receive healing. A woman in the rear portion of the tabernacle shouted in excitement. After a time of rejoicing in the Lord, the service continued. After the service a young lady made her way to the pulpit and asked if I had heard someone scream in the back of the tabernacle.

"I certainly did."

"That was my mother," she said. "Mother had a growth on her side the size of your fist. She lifted her hands to worship and then felt for the growth and it was gone."

God confirmed His Word with a miracle of healing. The woman believed and it happened. Faith was created by the Word. God "sent His word, and healed" (Psalm 107:20).

Pentecostal preaching has always produced miraculous results.

A beautiful example of the power of preaching to evoke faith is seen during the first missionary journey of Paul and Barnabas to Lystra.

> And there sat a certain man at Lystra, impotent in his feet, being a cripple from his mother's womb, who never had walked: The same heard Paul speak: who steadfastly beholding him, and perceiving that he had faith to be healed, Said with a loud voice, Stand upright on thy feet. And he leaped and walked (Acts 14:8-10).

When one reads this passage carefully, at least two miraculous things are seen to be taking place. While Paul is preaching, the man's faith builds to a peak: "the same heard Paul speak" (v. 9). This was faith of an unusual nature. It was divine faith, immediate faith, miracle faith produced by the Word. At the same time, Paul perceived the man had faith to believe. Paul discerned this supernaturally, through the Holy Spirit— not with human ingenuity, not with human understanding, but through and by the power of the Holy Ghost. The two miracles coalesced. They merged into a triumphant moment that brought immediate results. Though he had never walked before, the man leaped to his feet and walked.

Pentecostal preaching produces just such faith today.

It is a rewarding experience to see faces light up with expectation as faith is created by the preached Word. One can sense that listeners believe the Word and are willing to act upon it.

It has been this author's pleasure to see faith come alive in many hearts during the preaching of God's Word. One such occasion was while ministering during camp meeting at Beckley, West Virginia, on the "Gifts of the Spirit." I perceived that a woman in the audience had faith to receive the Baptism. When I paused to recognize her desire, the Spirit fell upon her as she sat in the pew.

It is through faith produced by the Word that signs and miracles follow Pentecostal preaching. These signs, in turn, confirm the Word just as Jesus insisted they would in the Gospel of Mark. Miracles, signs, wonders, mighty works—these are not in themselves the objectives of Pentecostal preaching; but they are evidences, proofs, witnesses to the power and authenticity of the eternal Word.

Pentecostal Preaching Confronts Demonic Powers

This world is in rebellion against God. There can be no compromise between righteousness and wickedness. While one sees evidence of this conflict on many levels, none is more clearly exposed than when the anointed preacher speaks as God's voice. For this reason, the Pentecostal minister may as well recognize that true preaching will inevitably conflict with entrenched powers and interests of this world.

Anointed Pentecostal preaching places the man of God in an unusual position. He feels the message burning in his heart, he knows what the Spirit bids him say, he may even realize that his words are being opposed by some outside power or being; nevertheless, the man of God preaches. He speaks forth the commandments and the directives of God and leaves the spiritual confrontation to the Holy Spirit. This explains why the preacher sometimes finds himself in a conflict he did not realize was coming, or why emergencies are both created and taken care of without his conscious knowledge.

One familiar example of this is found in Acts 7, occasioned by the preaching of Stephen. This original deacon of the church was powerfully anointed of the Holy Spirit. Stephen applied God's message white-hot to those who heard him, and it was the cutting sharpness of what he said that disturbed their evil hearts. Note the mob's reaction:

> When they heard these things, they were cut to the heart, and they gnashed on him with their teeth. . . . Then they cried out with a loud voice, and stopped their ears, and ran upon him with one accord, And cast him out of the city, and stoned him (vv. 54, 57, 58).

Yet another example concerns Paul's preaching at Ephesus and the resulting conflict between the gospel and the silversmiths (see 19:23-41). Paul's preaching impacted the city so dramatically that the silversmiths were hurt financially. Demetrius, apparently the leader of the silversmiths, called together other members of the guild, saying,

> Not only this our craft is in danger to be set at nought; but also that the temple of the great goddess Diana should be despised, and her magnificence should be destroyed, whom all Asia and the world worshippeth. And when they heard these sayings, they were full of wrath (vv. 27, 28).

We understand that there is but one God and that the goddess Diana was, as are all idols, but the work of men's hands. At the same time, we know demonic powers become involved in idol worship and that Satan stirs up this type opposition because he opposes any worship of the true God. "We wrestle not against flesh and blood, but against principalities, against powers, against the rulers of the darkness of this world, against spiritual wickedness in high places" (Ephesians 6:12).

Pentecostal preaching—anointed preaching that is empowered by the Holy Spirit—will stir up opposition. It will upset economic and social orders. It will conflict with established patterns and habits. Such is to be expected. However, the Pentecostal preacher must not cease preaching. This is what the hireling would do. God's man must continue to proclaim the Word, and this preaching will bring victory of a miraculous nature.

Pentecostal Preaching Produces Godly Fear and Respect for the Church

The Bible makes it clear, following the death of Ananias and Sapphira, that "great fear came upon all the church, and upon as many as heard these things. And by the hands of the apostles were many signs and wonders wrought among the people" (Acts 5:11, 12).

While it is not our purpose here to give a rationale for signs and miracles, it does seem obvious that God uses them as one method by which to enter human lives. Such marvelous things have taken place in the wake of Pentecostal preaching that an entire town has become stirred.

The effectiveness of such preaching is not in words alone, but rather in the listener's perception of what God is saying and doing at the moment. When the Word is preached uncompromisingly, when the Word goes forth with power and under the anointing of the Holy Spirit, people will develop an awesome respect for things spiritual. This is the soil from which come miracles and transformed lives.

Pentecostal Preaching Is Confirmed by Operation of Spiritual Gifts

In writing to the church at Corinth, Paul instructed believers to "covet earnestly the best gifts" (1 Corinthians 12:31). When one places this statement alongside what follows in chapter 13—Paul's "more excellent way"—and when these two passages are viewed within the context of the first part of chapter 12 and with chapter 14, balance is achieved. Paul did not wish the church to ignore or forget spiritual gifts, as some tend to do today, nor did he wish spiritual gifts to become an end in themselves. In fact, Paul clearly profiles the error of the latter choice. Instead, Paul wished the church to realize that the operation of spiritual gifts goes hand in hand with the preaching and teaching of God's Word.

As noted earlier, a key ingredient in Pentecostal preaching is prophecy. Under the anointing of the Holy Spirit, God's men prophesy—they "speak forth"—the things which are of God. Prophecy is a key operation of the Holy Spirit, one of the nine spiritual gifts (see 1 Corinthians 12:8-10). Prophecy is a gift that may be further confirmed by the operation of other gifts, all of which should be accepted as the natural result of Pentecostal preaching.

Some men express concern that the gifts of the Spirit do not operate in their churches today precisely as they feel they should. This may be a legitimate concern, one that should send the pastor into a period of prayer and fasting in search of God's will. However, the preacher should preach the Word. He should concentrate on becoming a holy instrument and on knowing the Spirit's directives. When this is faithfully followed, he will discover more and more that free flow of the Spirit which will in turn produce a genuine operation of spiritual gifts. When the Word is preached with the right attitude, and under Pentecostal anointing, spiritual gifts will naturally confirm God's word.

When God's men give themselves totally to setting forth what "thus saith the Lord," believers will mature spiritually. Lives will become more sensitive to the Holy Spirit, and the congregation will become in truth a Pentecostal church where all gifts operate in balance and in accordance with the spiritual order outlined in the Scriptures.

Summary

While society—the world, the face of this present generation—may seem to change, and while new challenges and new obstacles are placed in the way of those who seek righteousness on this earth, the perennial conflict between good and evil rages on. In this respect at least, our world has not changed at all. God still reigns supreme in the universe; Satan still opposes Him. God still moves in the hearts and lives of men and women, redeeming them through His grace and directing them into service through His Spirit; Satan still opposes His work in every way possible.

It is the man of God, the called and anointed preacher, who bears the brunt of this conflict. Upon the shoulders of this man rest tremendous responsibilities, upon the shoulders of this man, through the Holy Spirit, rest miraculous and supernatural powers. Since it is the gospel which is "the power of God unto salvation" (Romans 1:16), and since God has chosen through "the foolishness of preaching" (1 Corinthians 1:21) to bring men and women to a knowledge of the truth, it follows that those who are called of God should give top priority to preaching.

It is this emphasis that *Pentecostal Preaching* has tried to make. Preaching the gospel of Jesus Christ is not merely a task, not just something which one may or may not do: it is a divine commission, with heavy responsibility and with eternal rewards.

Equally important is our emphasis that a man preaches as he ought—a man preaches with power and authority, with honor and success—only when he follows the New Testament pattern. This means Pentecostal preaching as demonstrated on the Day of Pentecost and throughout the Book of Acts. The New Testament pattern of preaching means Pentecostal preaching that is precise, productive and prophetic; it is unique preaching which produces the same signs and wonders, the same miracles and revivals, the same marvelous results as found described in the Book of Acts.

The preacher's task in today's world has not changed: God has not changed. God still calls men to engage in conflict with evil. He still equips men with the power and the authority of His Spirit to do the job. Reason dictates that if one of these sentences be true, then the other must also be true. If our task today is the same as that which the New Testament church faced, then our equipment and spiritual power must be the same.

The man or woman of God who is called and anointed of the Holy Spirit, and who will faithfully yield to the leading of the Spirit, has the same commission and enablement as was given to the disciples of old.

Simply stated, this has been our thesis. It may not be one with which every reader agrees and it may not be one fully explained, but it is one that is the honest opinion of this author's heart.

Just as in the Book of Acts and within the New Testament church, Pentecostal preaching today will produce signs and wonders. It will change lives and bring revival. Pentecostal preaching is totally adequate for doing the task God has commissioned us to do in this day.